gourmet LOW CARB

gourmet LOW CARB

hamlyn

Sara Lewis

First published in Great Britain in 2005 by
Hamlyn, a division of Octopus Publishing Group Ltd
2–4 Heron Quays, London E14 4JP

Copyright © Octopus Publishing Group Ltd 2005

All rights reserved. No part of this work may be
reproduced or utilized in any form or by any means,
electronic or mechanical, including photocopying,
recording or by any information storage and
retrieval system, without the prior written
permission of the publisher.

ISBN 0 600 61348 8
EAN 9780600613480

A CIP catalogue record for this book is available
from the British Library

Printed and bound in China

10 9 8 7 6 5 4 3 2 1

Notes

Nutritional analyses are given per serving. Where a recipe
has split servings (e.g. 'serves 6–8'), the analysis is given
for the first figure.

The Department of Health advises that eggs should not
be consumed raw. This book contains some dishes made
with raw or lightly cooked eggs. It is prudent for more
vulnerable people, such as pregnant and nursing mothers,
invalids, the elderly, babies, and young children, to avoid
uncooked or lightly cooked dishes made with eggs.

Both metric and imperial measurements have been
given. Use one set of measurements only, and not a
mixture of both.

Standard level spoon measurements are used in all recipes.
1 tablespoon = one 15 ml spoon
1 teaspoon = one 5 ml spoon

Fresh herbs should be used unless otherwise stated.

Medium eggs should be used unless otherwise stated.

Ovens should be preheated to the specified temperature –
if using a fan-assisted oven, follow the manufacturer's
instructions for adjusting the time and the temperature.

CONTENTS

Introduction 6

Brilliant Brunches 16

Scintillating Starters and Sizzling Sides 38

Majestic Mains 70

Delightful Desserts 112

Index 142
Acknowledgements 144

INTRODUCTION

Carbohydrates have been causing a bit of a stir in the last few years as they have been linked to numerous diet fads and eating regimes, particularly among celebrities. However, as with any popular weight-loss programme, it is often the negative points that are highlighted, and basic nutritional information tends to be sidelined as people abuse diets and take them to the extreme.

Like any successful diet plan, a low-carb diet is really all about sensible eating – good food in abundance and bad food in moderation. The body needs a wide variety of foods to function effectively, and if you deprive your body of any essential food group you risk damaging your health. Carbohydrates are a source of energy for our bodies – a bit like the equivalent of petrol in a car. They fill us up and act as a fuel, keeping us going throughout the day.

There are many misconceptions surrounding the interpretation of the low-carb rule. The main one is that all carbohydrates are bad and should be avoided. In fact, there are actually two types of carbs – simple and complex – and it's the simple (or refined) carbohydrates that we should be cutting from our diets. Complex (or good) carbs have a vital part to play in our nutritional wellbeing and should be eaten in moderation as part of a well-balanced meal. Simple carbohydrates are basically sugars, including glucose from fruit, sucrose from sugar cane and lactose from milk. The reason these are bad is that most of our consumption of these sugars comes when they are part of refined or processed foods, such as ready meals, biscuits, cakes, carbonated drinks and some breakfast cereals. Complex carbohydrates, on the other hand, although they are made up of chains of sugars, are mainly starch based and include potatoes and other starchy vegetables, beans and pulses, grains and grain products that have undergone minimal processing (such as

brown bread and wholemeal pasta). When we look at the topic in these basic terms it's easy to see why complex carbohydrates can be beneficial to our health, while simple carbs are a real no-go.

The essential difference between 'good' and 'bad' carbs arises in the way they have been treated or processed before they become the food that we eat. Complex or unrefined carbohydrates are foods that remain in their natural, unprocessed state, thereby containing all the nutrients that our bodies require to break down into energy. Refined carbohydrates, which we consume in ready meals, crisps and cakes, provide virtually no nutritional benefits and are, in fact, detrimental to our health if they are eaten regularly. When food is highly processed, anything of nutritional value is stripped away, while the refined flour, sugar and processed fats that are left result in a rush of blood sugars in the body as the carbs are broken down into glucose. The body cannot

efficiently transfer all of this glucose into energy, so it is left with a glut of glucose, which is subsequently stored as fat. This imbalance in the body can have a long-term impact on health and may potentially lead to complications, such as type-2 diabetes or heart problems.

Eating the Right Carbs

Carbohydrates appear in every type of food, from fruit to chocolate, and to adjust your diet you need to understand which foods contain acceptable amounts of good carbs and which contain bad carbs and should be avoided altogether. Our bodies do not actually need refined carbohydrates, so, if possible, try to cut these out of your diet entirely or, at least, severely limit your intake of them. This may sound difficult, but it's possible to have an exciting and varied diet without resorting to ready meals and takeaways packed full of artificial additives. Meals consisting of refined carbohydrates may make you feel satisfied in the short term, but this often takes the form of a bloated stomach and a quick-fix sugar rush. Once these processed carbs have swiftly moved through your system, you will be left feeling hungry again but without having gained any nutritional benefit from your meal.

Complex carbohydrates are exactly that – complicated. Unlike refined carbs, they take longer to break down in your body, thus providing a steadier release of glucose and, because they retain all their original nutrients and haven't been processed, your body enjoys the benefits. One obvious change you can make is by switching from white to brown with many foods – white being processed or refined and brown being the more natural, complex version of the product. This rule applies to rice, pasta, bread and sugar among other foods, and although it's a good idea generally to limit your intake of bulky, carb-laden meals, if you switch to brown versions at least you'll be getting the maximum nutrients from your food. Raw or lightly cooked vegetables are another great source of good carbs, so try to increase your intake of these.

Switching to a low-carb diet doesn't mean that you'll have to forego luscious meals and special dinners – far from it. It is simply a way of categorizing food in terms of bad and good carbohydrates then trying to eliminate the former from your diet while reducing your intake of the latter. Once you become more aware of which foods are naturally low in carbohydrates and those that are beneficial to your health, it will become much easier to work around carbs when you are planning your meals. The recipes in this book are designed with functionality in mind. It's all very well embarking on a new eating regime, but it's a pointless exercise if it's impossible to recreate it every day, or if you find it too limiting or uninteresting. Low-carb meals can be as varied and elaborate as you want them to be, and when it comes to entertaining, your guests will be none the wiser about their low-carb meal unless you tell them.

The Glycaemic Index

The glycaemic index, or GI as it's more commonly known, is a system that measures the rate at which a particular food will be transferred into glucose and raise the blood sugar levels in your body and thereby whether it is good for you to eat or not. All carbohydrates take a different length of time to break down, and the GI index is a good indicator of whether certain carbs should be limited or eaten freely. Foods that raise blood sugar levels quickly (simple or refined carbohydrates) will have a high score, whereas those that break down more slowly and don't cause a peak in blood sugar (complex carbohydrates) will have a lower glycaemic index.

The GI of a food doesn't simply depend on whether it is a simple or complex carbohydrate, however. The other nutrients contained in that food also have an effect on its GI – some fruits and milk products would be classed as simple carbohydrates based on their sugar content, but these foods are actually a vital part of our diet because of the other nutritional components they contain. It's all about balance. If you imagine a

pyramid, these foods would appear towards the top, indicating that they should be included in the diet but in moderation.

A Healthy Approach

Common sense tells us that we should be cutting down on processed and refined foods and any foods that have a lot of sugar added to them. These foods are not only practically void in terms of nutritional benefits to the body, but they also promote weight gain, tooth decay, digestive problems and a propensity to develop type-2 diabetes. The less processed food you eat, the better it is going to be for you, and a low-carb diet will help to promote an overall feeling of better health and wellbeing. If you cut out the refined carbohydrates that are present in processed foods and cut back on portions of complex carbohydrates, you should soon notice an increase in your energy levels and concentration, and you should stop experiencing any severe transitions between feeling bloated one minute and having hunger pangs the next. A low-carb diet will iron out inconsistencies and can help you sleep better, too.

More important, perhaps, is the fact that you limit your risk of becoming overweight or even obese. Obesity is currently one of the biggest health issues facing the world as people, particularly in Western countries, continue to eat an increasing amount of processed food, such as takeaways, fizzy drinks and sugary snacks. This poor diet, with its high fat and sugar content, can also lead to clogged arteries and the subsequent risk of heart disease – a major killer in our society. However, it's no easy matter to change people's attitudes to their eating habits, and although we're all generally more aware of what we should and shouldn't be eating these days, as fast food becomes ever more widely available, it seems that governments may well have a full-scale food battle on their hands.

Maintaining the Low-carb Lifestyle

The low-carb diet isn't rigid or restrictive, and following it won't feel like some constant punishment for any previous unhealthy eating patterns. It's really all about making a few important changes to your basic eating habits, many of which should become obvious once you've delved into this book a little more. Everything you eat has an effect on your body to a certain degree, so it makes sense to eat more of the things that are good for you. Unlike other diets, the low-carb diet

doesn't mean you suddenly have to decline dinner invitations or pack away the best dinner plates because you won't be able to host a dinner party ever again. You'll still be able to enjoy meals out and invite friends round. As the recipes that follow demonstrate, there's nothing unglamorous or boring about the low-carb diet. There are endless possibilities for dishes, and you'll discover that by combining certain foods

you actually improve their effectiveness in terms of nutritional intake and fat burning.

Swap your processed breakfast cereal for a bowl of porridge and a banana. Choose soup instead of sandwiches for lunch. Snack on fruit and nuts instead of crisps and biscuits. Give pasta the elbow at dinner and opt for dishes that contain fish or chicken combined with fresh vegetables. Obviously, it's not quite as straightforward as that. Some vegetables are better than others, and some foods that are not great on the carb front in theory suddenly become a lot better for you if you serve them as part of a meal. Ultimately, your body will soon let you know if you're doing the right thing – many people don't even realize that their love of carbs is having a detrimental effect on their health until they cut down and feel the benefits. Weight loss, an increase in energy levels and no heavy, bloated feeling after a meal are just some positive points that may result from switching to a low-carb diet.

A Recipe for Success

You'll probably find that you don't have to alter your lifestyle and eating habits as much as you might think to make a real difference to your health. If you make small changes to your diet and substitute just a few foods for

healthier alternatives, you should soon start to notice the difference. Eating slow-burning foods will prolong your energy levels and make you feel brighter and happier generally and, best of all, you can still enjoy all the good things about eating.

Of course, it's all very well eating healthy foods and knowing more about the benefits of carb reduction, but you need to combine these changes to your diet with a programme of regular exercise if you are really to achieve a wholly healthy lifestyle. Exercise isn't just about weight loss and toning muscles: it's about your overall wellbeing.

A brisk walk or a jog will blow away the cobwebs, get your heart working and blood pumping, increase your metabolism and rid your body of lethargy. So make your decision to switch to a low-carb diet as part of a complete health makeover and your body will thank you for it.

CREATING A LOW-CARB MENU

Devising a low-carb menu isn't as difficult as it sounds, and there's no more work involved than in planning a normal dinner party or meal. There are recipes in this book for all kinds of occasions, from family meals to elegant dinner parties, and plenty of proof that 'gourmet' and 'low carb' are words that really can appear next to each other.

There are a few points to bear in mind when you're planning meals that will immediately put you on the right track, and, even though you might not be able to stick to these rules all the time, it's a good idea to bear them in mind before you even think about starting to prepare a meal.

- No sugar or white flour! If sugar is absolutely essential, use unrefined brown sugar, granulated sweeteners or honey instead.

- Try to decrease portion sizes. It's easy to pour a bit extra of everything into the pan when you're cooking 'just in case there's not enough', but you should carefully measure everything and not load up plates with too much food.

- When you're making a curry or chilli, serve it with brown rice instead of white and limit the amount you prepare. You can always serve an extra vegetable side dish if necessary.

- Always read the label! Food labels clearly state the amount of carbs and sugar a product contains, so try to work your meal around this and don't include too many high-carb ingredients.

- If pasta is a favourite for dinner, try to eat chicken, fish or meat accompanied

by plenty of fibre-rich vegetables instead. If you do serve pasta, restrict it to a side helping and always choose wholemeal types.

- If you love bread, give up over-processed white and eat granary or wholegrain. The same applies at mealtimes – serve wholegrain bread rolls or simply give the bread basket a miss.

- Serve natural low-fat yogurt or crème fraîche with desserts instead of ice cream or sugary sauces and always use fresh fruit instead of canned.

- If one element of a party menu is higher in carbs than you'd like, make sure the other courses bring the average down. You won't need too much extra planning for this, and you can pick out any combination of recipes in this book (see opposite for some menu suggestions), so there are plenty of options.

MENU SUGGESTIONS

Meal for two

CITRUS-DRESSED ASPARAGUS
with Smoked Salmon and Quail Eggs
(see page 29) – make up one-third of the recipe

CREAMY LOBSTER
with Shallots and Vermouth (see page 80)
– make up half quantity

BITTER CHOCOLATE MOUSSE
with Chilli and Cinnamon (see page 128)
– freeze the remaining 4 portions for another time

TOTAL CARBS 27 g per person

Family supper for 4

CHICKEN TIKKA STICKS
with Fennel Raita (see page 62)
– eat left over portions the following day

AUBERGINE AND ALMOND ROULADES
with Garlicky Tomato Sauce (see page 104)

MINTED ZABAGLIONE
with Blueberries (see page 124)
– with 2 extra portions for seconds

TOTAL CARBS 33 g per person
– without pudding seconds

Birthday breakfast for 6

MELON TRIO
with Green Tea Infusion (see page 34)

EGGS EN COCOTTE
with Tomatoes, Salmon and Tarragon
(see page 21)

TOTAL CARBS 22 g per person

Summer lunch al fresco for 6

BAKED FIGS
with Minted Picon Cheese (see page 32)
– make up half as much again to serve 6

SEARED SALMON
with Vietnamese Salad (see page 72)

PIMM'S JELLIES
with Iced Lemonade (see page 126)

TOTAL CARBS 30 g per person

Winter warmer for 6

DU BARRY SOUP
with Parmesan Thins (see page 52)

DAUBE OF BEEF
with Mushrooms and Pancetta (see page 86)

NEEP BREE
with Grated Ginger (see page 49)

MINI ALMOND ANGEL CAKES
with Berry Fruits (see page 140)

TOTAL CARBS 34 g per person

Sunday lunch for 4

GINGER SCALLOPS
with Asparagus (see page 59)

RACK OF LAMB
with Baba Ghanoush (see page 90)

TIPSY BLUEBERRY POTS
with Mascarpone (see page 137)

TOTAL CARBS 29 g per person

After work supper with friends for 6

MISO BROTH
with Prawns (see page 54)

GRILLED SALMON
with Leek and Pancetta Confetti
(see page 74)

SEARED PINEAPPLE
with Hot Plum Sauce (see page 118)

TOTAL CARBS 32 g per person

ESSENTIAL INFORMATION

Low-carb eating isn't just a diet, it's a whole lifestyle, and the changes you make should be long-term ones. However, that doesn't mean a regime of dull meals and a ban on nights out. Follow our quick-reference guidelines below for information on shopping, entertaining and everyday living and you'll soon find that thinking on low-carb lines has become part of your daily life.

Shopping

BUY

- Fresh fruit such as apples, bananas and oranges
- Fresh vegetables, especially green vegetables
- Dried fruits and nuts (but check labels for added ingredients)
- Lean meat and fish
- Natural porridge oats, wholegrain and granary bread
- Brown rice
- Pulses and beans

WALK PAST

- Processed breakfast cereals, white bread and other white flour products
- White rice and pasta
- Rich cooking sauces, dips and salad dressings
- Processed ready meals, sugary snacks, crisps
- Processed meat products
- Chocolate
- Fizzy drinks

SHOPPING TIPS

- Buy some fresh frozen veg so that you'll always have healthy, low-carb ingredients to hand.
- Check the label before putting anything in your shopping trolley.
- Roughly plan your meals before shopping and make a list so that you don't get sidetracked.
- Opt for organic foods wherever possible.

Cooking

- Make double the amount of certain dishes and freeze the remainder – great for busy days when you have no time or initiative to cook from scratch.

- Keep oil and cooking fat to a minimum by grilling, griddling or steaming food.

- Make your own sauces for chicken, fish or rice – the bought varieties tend to be higher in carbs.

- Start meals with a salad – it's healthy and will limit the amount eaten after.

- Choose lean cuts of meat, or trim all excess fat before cooking.

- Include more fish in your diet.

Eating out

- Opt for a side salad instead of a starter and ask for dressing on the side.

- Pass on the bread basket.

- Choose a vegetable side dish rather than mashed potato or fries.

- Try to pick well-balanced meals that aren't dominated by rich sauces.

- Choose fruit-based desserts.

- Opt for decaf coffee or a mint or fruit tea for an after-dinner drink.

Entertaining

- Serve crudités and tomato-based dips for nibbles instead of crisps.

- Try not to serve the food too late – it's better to eat earlier on in the evening.

- Keep starters simple and base them around low-carb ingredients – avocado, asparagus or smoked salmon are all delicious but simple options – and allow guests to serve their own sauce.

TIPS FOR SUCCESS

- Don't fall foul of unhealthy snacking – if you only keep healthy snacks in the cupboard you won't be tempted by crisps or chocolate. Nuts, dried fruit, apples, bananas and low-fat yogurts are just some of the healthier alternatives.

- Always eat breakfast – it gets your metabolism working and is an opportunity to eat some fresh fruit or low-fat yogurt.

- Home-made soups or substantial salads (made with pulses, tuna, egg, etc.) make good sandwich alternatives for lunchtime.

- Allow yourself a treat every so often – you're more likely to fail if you're too strict on your eating regime.

Brilliant Brunches

PRAWNS
with Piri-Piri

Piri-piri seasoning is a Portuguese chilli-based spice blend made with tiny piri-piri chillies from Africa. Look out for jars of it alongside the other spices in the supermarket and try adding it to a marinade for fresh sardines.

Preparation time 15 mins, plus chilling

Cooking time 5–6 mins

Serves 6

3 tablespoons olive oil

grated rind and juice of 1 lemon

2 teaspoons piri-piri seasoning

2 teaspoons tomato purée

2 garlic cloves, finely chopped

400 g (13 oz) raw, headless shell-on tiger prawns, (thawed if frozen)

salt and pepper

GARNISH

chopped parsley

lemon wedges

CARBOHYDRATE 1 g

FAT 6 g

PROTEIN 12 g

ENERGY 104 kcal/433 kJ

1 Mix the oil, lemon rind and juice, piri-piri seasoning, tomato purée and garlic in a shallow bowl with a little salt and pepper.

2 Put the prawns in a sieve, rinse under cold running water and drain well. Add the prawns to the piri-piri mixture and toss until evenly coated. Cover with clingfilm and chill for at least 2 hours.

3 When you are ready to serve, thread the prawns on to 12 skewers through the thickest part of the body and tail and arrange them on a foil-lined grill rack.

4 Cook the prawns under a preheated grill for 5–6 minutes, turning them once, until they are bright pink. Arrange on a serving plate, sprinkle with chopped parsley and garnish with lemon wedges.

TIP If using wooden skewers, don't forget to soak them in water for 30 minutes before you need them.

PIPERADE
with Pastrami

A popular Basque dish, this gourmet-style scrambled eggs has a tomato and pepper sauce base, known as sofrito, which can be prepared in advance. Cook the eggs at the last moment for best results and serve with slices of pastrami, Bayonne or Parma ham.

Preparation time 20 mins

Cooking time 25 mins

Serves 6

6 large eggs

sprigs of fresh thyme, leaves removed, or large pinch of dried thyme, plus extra sprigs to garnish

1 tablespoon olive oil

125 g (4 oz) pastrami, thinly sliced

salt and pepper

SOFRITO

375 g (12 oz) or 3 small, different coloured peppers

1 tablespoon olive oil

1 Spanish onion, finely chopped

2 garlic cloves, crushed

500 g (1 lb) tomatoes, skinned, deseeded and chopped

CARBOHYDRATE 9 g

FAT 11 g

PROTEIN 14 g

ENERGY 186 kcal/776 kJ

1 Make the sofrito. Grill or cook the peppers directly in a gas flame for about 10 minutes, turning them until the skins have blistered and blackened. Rub the skins from the flesh and discard. Rinse the peppers under cold running water. Halve and deseed and cut the flesh into strips.

2 Heat the oil in a large frying pan, add the onion and cook gently for 10 minutes until softened and transparent. Add the garlic, tomatoes and peppers and simmer for 5 minutes until any juice has evaporated from the tomatoes. Set aside until ready to serve.

3 Beat the eggs with the thyme and salt and pepper in a bowl. Reheat the tomato mixture. Heat the oil in a saucepan, add the eggs, stirring until they are lightly scrambled. Stir into the reheated sofrito and spoon on to plates. Arrange slices of pastrami around the eggs and serve immediately, garnished with a little extra thyme.

TIP If you prefer, mix fried sliced chorizo sausage into the piperade instead of serving it with slices of cold pastrami.

EGGS EN COCOTTE
with Tomatoes, Salmon and Tarragon

These glamorous-sounding breakfast eggs are quick and easy to assemble and can be left to cook gently in the oven while you enjoy a leisurely glass of chilled fruit juice or sparkling buck's fizz.

Preparation time 15 mins
Cooking time 8–10 mins
Serves 6

25 g (1 oz) butter, for greasing
100 g (3½ oz) sun-blushed tomatoes, chopped
250 g (8 oz) salmon fillet, skinned and thinly sliced
6 large eggs
200 ml (7 fl oz) double cream
4 teaspoons chopped tarragon, plus extra to garnish
salt and pepper
wholegrain toast, to serve
watercress, to garnish

CARBOHYDRATE 2 g
FAT 31 g
PROTEIN 16 g
ENERGY 348 kcal/1440 kJ

1 Butter 6 shallow ovenproof dishes and set them in 2 large roasting tins. Add the tomatoes and salmon slices around the edges of the dishes and carefully break an egg into the centre of each one.

2 Mix together the cream and tarragon. Pour the mixture over and around the eggs, taking care that you do not completely cover the yolks. Sprinkle with a little salt and pepper.

3 Pour boiling water into the roasting tins to come halfway up the sides of the dishes. Bake, uncovered, in a preheated oven, 180°C (350°F), Gas Mark 4, for 8–10 minutes until the eggs are just set and the salmon is cooked through. Garnish with a little extra chopped tarragon and serve with fingers of wholegrain toast and a few sprigs of watercress.

TIP For vegetarian guests omit the salmon and add sliced mushrooms instead.

MOROCCAN BAKED EGGS
on Red Vegetables

This is a substantial dish, suitable for a late breakfast or Sunday brunch. The eggs should only be lightly cooked so that the yolks will flow over the vegetables.

Preparation time 10 mins
Cooking time 35 mins
Serves 4

5 tablespoons olive oil
1 Spanish onion, sliced
4 garlic cloves, crushed
4 red peppers, cored, deseeded and sliced
1 courgette, sliced
5 tomatoes, sliced
2 tablespoons chopped parsley
large pinch of paprika
large pinch of dried chilli flakes
4 eggs
salt and pepper

GARNISH
ground cumin
paprika
4 sprigs of coriander

CARBOHYDRATE 14 g
FAT 21 g
PROTEIN 10 g
ENERGY 279 kcal/1157 kJ

1 Heat the oil in a large frying pan. Add the onion and fry briskly until golden. Add the garlic, peppers, courgette and tomatoes and simmer for 15–20 minutes, stirring occasionally, until all the vegetables are soft.

2 Stir in the parsley, paprika and chilli flakes and season to taste. Simmer for a further 5 minutes.

3 Spoon the vegetable mixture into a large, shallow, ovenproof dish. Make 4 indentations in the vegetable mixture and break an egg into each one. Bake in a preheated oven, 160°C (325°F), Gas Mark 3, for 10 minutes until the egg whites are just set but the yolks are still runny.

4 Before serving, sprinkle ground cumin and paprika over the eggs and garnish with the coriander.

COURGETTE FRITTATAS
with Mint

These little frittatas, speckled with mint, are cooked in a deep muffin tin rather than the more traditional frying pan. They are served with a tomato sauce with a hint of garlic.

Preparation time 10 mins
Cooking time about 30 mins
Serves 6

TOMATO SAUCE

1 tablespoon olive oil

1 onion, finely chopped

1–2 garlic cloves, crushed (optional)

500 g (1 lb) plum tomatoes, chopped

FRITTATA

1 tablespoon olive oil

1 onion, finely chopped

2 courgettes, about 375 g (12 oz) in total, halved lengthways and thinly sliced

6 eggs

300 ml (½ pint) semi-skimmed milk

3 tablespoons grated Parmesan cheese

2 tablespoons chopped mint, plus extra leaves to garnish (optional)

salt and pepper

CARBOHYDRATE 11 g
FAT 12 g
PROTEIN 12 g
ENERGY 200 kcal/834 kJ

1 Make the sauce. Heat the oil in a saucepan, stir in the onion and fry for 5 minutes, stirring occasionally until softened and just beginning to brown. Add the garlic, if using, the tomatoes and salt and pepper. Stir and simmer for 5 minutes until the tomatoes are soft. Purée in a liquidizer or food processor until smooth, sieve into a bowl and keep warm.

2 Make the frittatas. Heat the oil in a frying pan, add the onion and fry until softened and just beginning to brown. Add the courgettes, stir to combine and cook for 3–4 minutes until softened but not browned.

3 Divide the courgette mixture among 12 greased sections of a deep muffin tin. Beat together the eggs, milk, Parmesan and mint. Season well and pour over the courgette mixture in the muffin tin. Bake in a preheated oven, 190°C (375°F), Gas Mark 5, for about 15 minutes until they are lightly browned and well risen and the egg mixture has set.

4 Leave in the tin for 1–2 minutes then loosen the edges with a knife. Turn out and arrange on plates with the warm tomato sauce. Garnish with extra mint leaves, if liked.

TIP The tomato sauce can be made the day before and kept in the refrigerator.

SAUTÉED KIDNEYS
with Tomatoes and Marsala

Preparation time 20 mins

Cooking time 20–23 mins

Serves 6

25 g (1 oz) butter

1 tablespoon olive oil

1 onion, thinly sliced

10 lambs' kidneys, cored and trimmed

375 g (12 oz) cherry tomatoes, halved

1 teaspoon Dijon mustard

1 teaspoon tomato purée

200 ml (7 fl oz) Marsala

8 rashers of streaky bacon

50 g (2 oz) wild rocket leaves

4 teaspoons balsamic vinegar

3 slices of wholegrain bread

salt and pepper

CARBOHYDRATE 13 g

FAT 16 g

PROTEIN 19 g

ENERGY 303 kcal/1267 kJ

1 Heat the butter and oil in a frying pan, add the onion and cook for 5 minutes until softened and lightly browned. Add the kidneys and fry over a high heat for 3 minutes until browned.

2 Add the tomatoes and cook for 2 minutes, then stir in the mustard, tomato purée, Marsala and salt and pepper. Cook for 2–3 minutes, stirring, until the sauce has reduced slightly and the kidneys are cooked. Cover with a lid and keep hot.

3 Wind the bacon around 8 metal skewers and grill for 8–10 minutes until crisp. Toss the rocket leaves in the vinegar. Toast the bread and cut each slice in half.

4 Arrange the toast on serving plates, reheat the kidneys if necessary and spoon them on to the toast. Slide the skewers from the bacon and arrange the bacon attractively on the kidneys. Spoon the rocket salad to the side and serve immediately.

BUCKWHEAT CRÊPES
with Ricotta, Smoked Salmon and Artichokes

These delicate buckwheat crêpes are drizzled into the frying pan with a spoon rather than a ladle to create a filigree or lace doily effect with less batter and so fewer carbs.

Preparation time 20 mins

Cooking time 15 mins

Serves 6

BATTER

100 g (3½ oz) buckwheat flour

1 egg

250 ml (8 fl oz) semi-skimmed milk

FILLING

125 g (4 oz) ricotta cheese

3 tablespoons chopped parsley or parsley and basil mixed, plus extra basil leaves to garnish

1 small garlic clove, crushed (optional)

grated rind of ½ lemon and juice of 1 lemon

2 tablespoons sunflower oil

250 g (8 oz) smoked salmon, sliced

400 g (13 oz) can artichoke hearts, drained and quartered

salt and pepper

CARBOHYDRATE 19 g

FAT 10 g

PROTEIN 19 g

ENERGY 229 kcal/958 kJ

1 Make the batter. Put the flour, egg, a little of the milk and some salt into a bowl and whisk until smooth. Gradually whisk in the remaining milk.

2 Make the filling. Mix the ricotta with the herbs, garlic, if using, and lemon rind and season gently.

3 Heat a little of the oil in a nonstick frying pan. When it is hot pour the excess into a small, heatproof bowl. Drizzle in 3 tablespoons of the batter to make lacy crêpes about 18 cm (7 inches) in diameter, then cook until the underside is browned. Loosen with a palette knife, turn over and cook the other side in the same way. Lift the crêpe out on to a plate and keep warm. Make 5 more in the same way, adding more oil if needed.

4 Arrange each crêpe on a serving plate, divide the ricotta filling among them and top them with strips of smoked salmon and artichoke quarters. Drizzle with lemon juice and sprinkle with pepper. Fold the crêpes over the filling and garnish with some extra chopped herbs.

TIP The crêpes can be made earlier in the day and kept, interleaved with nonstick baking paper and wrapped loosely with foil. Reheat in a preheated oven, 190°C (375°F), Gas Mark 5, for 5 minutes.

OATMEAL AND MUSTARD-CRUSTED HERRING
with Roasted Cherry Tomatoes

A crisp oatmeal crust speckled with wholegrain mustard traps all the moist flavour of this underrated fish, which is rich in omega oils.

Preparation time 15 mins

Cooking time 12 mins

Serves 6

6 herrings, gutted weight 175 g (6 oz) each, cut into fillets

3 teaspoons wholegrain mustard

6 tablespoons medium oatmeal

500 g (1 lb) cherry tomatoes on the vine

1 tablespoon olive oil

25 g (1 oz) butter

3 rashers of back bacon, diced (optional)

salt and pepper

sprigs of flat leaf parsley, to garnish (optional)

CARBOHYDRATE 12 g

FAT 41 g

PROTEIN 34 g

ENERGY 552 kcal/2294 kJ

1 Rinse the herring fillets in cold water and pat them dry with kitchen paper. Spread each side thinly with mustard then coat them in oatmeal.

2 Snip the tomatoes into 6 portions, leaving them on the vine, and put them in a roasting tin. Brush sparingly with oil and sprinkle with salt and pepper. Cook in a preheated oven, 200°C (400°F), Gas Mark 6, for 10 minutes.

3 Meanwhile, heat half the butter in a frying pan, add half the herring fillets and bacon, if using, and cook the fish for 2–3 minutes on each side until they are golden and flake easily when pressed with a knife. Transfer the herrings to a plate and keep hot in the bottom of the oven while you cook the rest in the same way.

4 Arrange 2 herring fillets on each serving plate, spooning any remaining pan juices around them. Add the roasted tomatoes and garnish with sprigs of flat leaf parsley, if liked.

CITRUS-DRESSED ASPARAGUS
with Smoked Salmon and Quail Eggs

Short of time? Impress your friends with this elegant starter, which is perfect for spring and early summer. It can be rustled up in a matter of minutes.

Preparation time 10 mins

Cooking time 6 mins

Serves 6

200 g (7 oz) trimmed asparagus

3 tablespoons roughly chopped hazelnuts

4 teaspoons olive oil

juice of 1 lime

1 teaspoon Dijon mustard

12 quail eggs

250 g (8 oz) smoked salmon

salt and pepper

CARBOHYDRATE 1 g

FAT 10 g

PROTEIN 15 g

ENERGY 150 kcal/624 kJ

1 Steam the asparagus spears over a pan of boiling water for 5 minutes until just tender.

2 Meanwhile, grill the nuts on a piece of foil until lightly browned. Lightly mix together the oil, lime juice and mustard with a little salt and pepper then stir in the hot nuts. Keep warm.

3 Pour water into a saucepan to a depth of 4 cm (1½ inches) and bring it to the boil. Lower the eggs into the water with a slotted spoon and cook for 1 minute. Take the pan off the heat and leave the eggs to stand for 1 minute. Drain the eggs, rinse with cold water and drain again.

4 Tear the salmon into slightly smaller strips and divide it among 6 serving plates, folding and twisting the strips attractively. Tuck the just-cooked asparagus into the salmon, halve the quail eggs, leaving the shells on if liked, and arrange on top. Drizzle with the warm nut dressing and serve sprinkled with a little black pepper.

TIP Parma or Serrano ham could be used instead of smoked salmon.

BEETROOT, RED ONION AND PUMPKIN BAKE
with Roasted Mini Goats' Cheese

Smarter and lower in carbs, this oven-baked version of potato hash browns is topped with creamy, just-melted goats' cheese and can be served not only for brunch but as a starter for a dinner party.

Preparation time 20 mins

Cooking time 25–30 mins

Serves 4

400 g (13 oz) raw beetroot, peeled and diced

625 g (1¼ lb) pumpkin or butternut squash, peeled, deseeded and cut into slightly larger dice

1 red onion, cut into wedges

2 tablespoons olive oil

2 teaspoons fennel seeds

2 small goats' cheeses, 100 g (3½ oz) each

salt and pepper

chopped rosemary, to garnish

CARBOHYDRATE 17 g

FAT 14 g

PROTEIN 10 g

ENERGY 230 kcal/963 kJ

1 Put the beetroot, pumpkin and onion into a roasting tin, drizzle with the oil and sprinkle with the fennel seeds and salt and pepper. Roast the vegetables in a preheated oven, 200°C (400°F), Gas Mark 6, for 20–25 minutes, turning once, until well browned and tender.

2 Cut the goats' cheeses in half and nestle each half among the roasted vegetables. Sprinkle the cheeses with a little salt and pepper and drizzle with some of the pan juices.

3 Return the dish to the oven for about 5 minutes, until the cheese is just beginning to melt. Sprinkle with rosemary and serve immediately.

TIP Get the vegetables ready a little in advance and drizzle them with the oil, fennel and flavourings, then put them into the oven when your guests arrive.

BAKED FIGS
with Minted Picon Cheese

Preparation time 10 mins

Cooking time 10 mins

Serves 4

8 fresh figs

juice and grated rind of ½ orange

100 g (3½ oz) blue picon cheese or creamy Gorgonzola, St Agur or dolcelatte

small bunch of mint, plus extra to garnish

8 slices Bayonne or Parma ham

CARBOHYDRATE 12 g

FAT 12 g

PROTEIN 16 g

ENERGY 219 kcal/917 kJ

1 Rinse the figs in cold water and drain. Make a cross-cut down through each fig, but not completely through the base. Open them out slightly and arrange in a shallow, ovenproof dish. Squeeze the orange juice into the centre of each fig.

2 Bake the figs in a preheated oven, 180°C (350°F), Gas Mark 4, for 5 minutes. Crumble the cheese into the centre of the figs and sprinkle a little torn mint over them. Bake for a further 5 minutes until the cheese has just melted and the figs are hot.

3 Transfer the figs to serving plates, spooning any cooking juices around them. Arrange folds of ham by the side and garnish with extra mint leaves and the grated orange rind.

MAPLE GLAZED GRANOLA
with Tropical Fruits and Yogurt

Home-made granola is infinitely superior to the sugary, shop-bought versions. Use this wonderfully crunchy topping to enhance a tropical fruit salad and serve with spoonfuls of mild, creamy yogurt or crème fraîche.

Preparation time 20 mins
Cooking time 5–8 mins
Serves 6

2 tablespoons olive oil
2 tablespoons maple syrup
40 g (1½ oz) flaked almonds
40 g (1½ oz) pine nuts
25 g (1 oz) sunflower seeds
25 g (1 oz) porridge oats
375 g (12 oz) low-fat natural yogurt

FRUIT SALAD
1 mango, pitted, peeled and sliced
2 kiwifruit, peeled and sliced
small bunch of red seedless grapes, halved
grated rind and juice of 1 lime

CARBOHYDRATE 22 g
FAT 15 g
PROTEIN 7 g
ENERGY 246 kcal/1028 kJ

1 Heat the oil in a flameproof frying pan with a metal handle, add the maple syrup and the nuts, seeds and oats and toss together.

2 Transfer the pan to a preheated oven, 180°C (350°F), Gas Mark 4, and cook for 5–8 minutes, stirring once and moving the brown edges to the centre, until the mixture is evenly toasted.

3 Leave the mixture to cool, then pack it into a storage jar, seal, label and use within 10 days.

4 Make the fruit salad. Mix the fruits with the lime rind and juice, spoon the mixture into dishes and top with spoonfuls of yogurt and granola.

TIP Make up your own fruit salad combinations, such as raspberries, strawberries and blueberries or green grapes, papaya and melon. The quantities for the granola can be doubled or tripled and stored in an airtight jar for up to 10 days.

MELON TRIO
with Green Tea Infusion

Green tea is known for its soothing, relaxing properties, and its delicate flavour perfectly complements the light perfume and freshness of the different melons.

Preparation time 15 mins, plus chilling

Cooking time none

Serves 6

2 orange-flavoured green teabags

300 ml (½ pint) boiling water

1 orange-fleshed cantaloupe melon, such as charentais

½ green-fleshed melon, such as galia or ogen

½ honeydew melon

2 tablespoons light cane sugar

grated rind and juice of 1 lime

DECORATION

lime wedges

6 fresh lychees

CARBOHYDRATE 20 g

FAT 0 g

PROTEIN 2 g

ENERGY 83 kcal/353 kJ

1 Put the teabags into a jug and pour the boiling water over them. Leave to infuse for 2 minutes. Lift out the bags, draining them well. Break open one of the bags, remove a few tea leaves and add them to the tea infusion. Leave to cool.

2 Halve the whole melon and scoop out the seeds. Remove the seeds from the other melons. Cut away the skin with a small knife and cut the orange- and green-fleshed melons into long, thin slices. Dice the honeydew melon. Put all the prepared melon into a large, shallow dish.

3 Sprinkle the sugar, lime rind and juice over the melon and pour over the tea. Cover with clingfilm and chill for 1 hour, or overnight if preferred.

4 Arrange the long melon slices in fan shapes on individual serving plates. Spoon the diced melon to the side of the melon fans and serve each one with lime wedges and a partially peeled lychee.

TIP Don't be tempted to leave the tea to infuse for longer than 2 minutes, or it will taste bitter.

CRANACHAN
with Raspberries

Preparation time 20 mins

Cooking time 5–8 mins

Serves 6

40 g (1½ oz) medium oatmeal

150 ml (¼ pint) whipping cream

200 g (7 oz) fromage frais

2 tablespoons thick-set honey, ideally lavender or another flower honey

250 g (8 oz) raspberries (just-thawed if frozen)

CARBOHYDRATE 16 g

FAT 13 g

PROTEIN 4 g

ENERGY 190 kcal/800 kJ

1 Put the oatmeal in a shallow baking tin and toast it in a preheated oven, 180°C (350°F), Gas Mark 4, for 5–8 minutes, stirring once until evenly browned. Leave to cool.

2 Whip the cream until it forms soft peaks. Fold in the fromage frais, then the honey and, finally, incorporate the cooled oatmeal.

3 Reserving a few raspberries to top the desserts, divide half the remaining raspberries among 6 small glass dishes. Spoon half the cream mixture on top, then repeat with the other raspberries and the remaining cream mixture. Arrange the reserved raspberries on top and chill until ready to serve.

TIP The oatmeal can be toasted well in advance, but it is best to mix it with the cream only at the last minute because oatmeal swells with standing.

BALSAMIC GRILLED MUSHROOM CUPS
with Gammon and Chive Scramble

This stylish version of eggs and bacon is made by topping a grilled gammon steak with a large flat field mushroom and softly cooked scrambled eggs flavoured with chopped chives and Dijon mustard.

Preparation time 15 minutes

Cooking time 8–10 minutes

Serves 4

4 large flat mushrooms, about 250 g (8 oz) in total

1 tablespoon olive oil

1 tablespoon balsamic vinegar

2 gammon steaks, each about 225 g (7 ½ oz)

6 eggs

4 tablespoons semi-skimmed milk

1 teaspoon Dijon mustard

4 tablespoons chopped chives, plus extra whole chives, to garnish

25 g (1 oz) butter

salt and pepper

CARBOHYDRATE 2 g

FAT 21 g

PROTEIN 33 g

ENERGY 330 kcal/1383 kJ

1 Peel the mushrooms and leave the stalks intact. Mix together the oil, vinegar and a little salt and pepper. Brush over the top and underside of each mushroom then put them into a grill pan. Halve the gammon steaks and add to the pan. Cook under a pre-heated grill for 8–10 minutes, turning once, until browned.

2 Meanwhile, fork together the eggs, milk, Dijon mustard and a little salt and pepper then mix in the chopped chives.

3 Heat the butter in a small nonstick saucepan, add the egg mixture and stir until lightly scrambled.

4 Quickly transfer the gammon steaks to serving plates, top each one with a mushroom then fill with the eggs. Garnish with extra whole chives and serve immediately.

Scintillating
Starters and
Sizzling Sides

MIXED LEAF
and Pomegranate Salad

Turn a simple green salad into something rather exotic by adding jewel-like, glistening, ruby red pomegranate seeds and the delicate sweetness of raspberry vinegar.

Preparation time 10 mins

Cooking time none

Serves 6

3 tablespoons raspberry vinegar

2 tablespoons light olive oil

1 pomegranate

125 g (4 oz) mixed salad leaves (including baby spinach leaves, red mustard and mizuna)

salt and pepper

fresh raspberries, to garnish (optional)

CARBOHYDRATE 1 g

FAT 4 g

PROTEIN 1 g

ENERGY 43 kcal/177 kJ

1 Put the raspberry vinegar, olive oil and a little salt and pepper into a salad bowl and mix lightly.

2 Cut the pomegranate in half, then break or cut it into large pieces and flex the skin so that the small red seeds fall out. Pick out any stubborn ones with a small knife and throw away, then add the remainder to the salad bowl, discarding the skin and pith.

3 Break any large salad leaves into bite-sized pieces and toss them in the dressing. Sprinkle with raspberries, if liked, and serve at once.

TIP Pomegranates can be squeezed on a lemon juicer. Mix the juice with a little olive or walnut oil and use it to marinate chicken or pheasant breasts before pan frying.

WARM COURGETTE
and Lime Salad

Preparation time 10 mins

Cooking time 10 mins

Serves 4

1 tablespoon olive oil

grated rind and juice of 1 lime

1 garlic clove, finely chopped

2 tablespoons roughly chopped coriander
leaves, plus extra to garnish

2 courgettes, about 325 g (11 oz) in total, cut
into thin diagonal slices

salt and pepper

CARBOHYDRATE 4 g

FAT 3 g

PROTEIN 1 g

ENERGY 47 kcal/194 kJ

1 Mix together the oil, lime rind and juice, garlic, chopped coriander and salt and pepper in a plastic bag. Add the courgette slices and toss in the oil mixture. Seal and set aside until ready to cook.

2 Heat a ridged frying pan. Arrange as many courgette slices as will fit in a single layer over the base of the pan and cook for 2–3 minutes until browned on the underside. Turn the slices over and brown on the second side then transfer them to a warmed serving dish while you cook the remaining courgettes in the same way.

3 Pour any remaining dressing over the courgettes, sprinkle with a little extra chopped coriander to garnish and serve immediately.

TIP Cook thin slices of aubergine in the same way.

CREAMY CELERIAC DAUPHINOISE
with Nutmeg and Garlic

Slices of blanched celeriac are bathed in a creamy sauce flavoured with spring onions and just a hint of nutmeg and garlic for a rich side dish that slashes the carbs of its potato counterpart. Delicious served with daube of beef or grilled fish.

Preparation time 15 mins

Cooking time 40–45 mins

Serves 6

1 celeriac, about 625 g (1¼ lb), peeled and thinly sliced

3 spring onions, thinly sliced

250 ml (8 fl oz) double cream

3 large garlic cloves, finely chopped

grated nutmeg

25 g (1 oz) butter

salt and pepper

CARBOHYDRATE 4 g

FAT 24 g

PROTEIN 2 g

ENERGY 238 kcal/980 kJ

1 Cook the sliced celeriac in a saucepan of boiling water for 3 minutes. Drain in a colander, rinse with cold water and drain again.

2 Layer the celeriac and spring onions in a lightly buttered ovenproof dish. Mix together the cream, garlic, nutmeg and salt and pepper and pour over the celeriac. Dot with butter, cover loosely with clingfilm and chill until ready to cook.

3 Remove the clingfilm and cook the dauphinoise in a preheated oven, 190°C (375°F), Gas Mark 5, for 30–35 minutes until browned on top and the celeriac slices are tender.

BAKED AUTUMN ROOTS
with Mixed Spices

The mix of butternut squash, parsnips and carrots is a tasty alternative to traditional roast potatoes and is much lower in carbohydrates. The spicy flavouring of fennel, cumin and coriander seeds, turmeric, paprika and garlic makes all the difference.

Preparation time 15 mins

Cooking time 35–40 mins

Serves 6

1 teaspoon fennel seeds

1 teaspoon cumin seeds

1 teaspoon coriander seeds

½ teaspoon turmeric

½ teaspoon paprika

2 garlic cloves, chopped

3 tablespoons olive oil

500 g (1 lb) butternut squash, peeled, halved, deseeded and thickly sliced

4 small parsnips, about 425 g (14 oz) in total, cut into quarters

3 carrots, about 300 g (10 oz) in total, cut into thick strips

salt and pepper

CARBOHYDRATE 20 g

FAT 7 g

PROTEIN 3 g

ENERGY 147 kcal/619 kJ

1 Crush the seeds using a pestle and mortar or use the end of a rolling pin. Transfer to a large plastic bag and add the turmeric, paprika, garlic, oil and salt and pepper. Squeeze the bag to mix together.

2 Add the vegetables to the plastic bag, grip the top edge to seal and toss together until the vegetables are coated with the spices.

3 Tip the vegetables into a roasting tin and bake in a preheated oven, 200°C (400°F), Gas Mark 6, for 35–40 minutes, turning once until browned and tender. Transfer to a serving dish.

BABY CARROTS
with Lime and Cardamom Butter

Make the herb butter and keep it in the refrigerator for up to two weeks until it's needed. The butter also tastes good with grilled fish or beef steaks.

Preparation time 10 mins
Cooking time 10–12 mins
Serves 6

4 cardamom pods
50 g (2 oz) butter
grated rind of 1 lime
pepper
400 g (13 oz) trimmed baby carrots

CARBOHYDRATE 4 g
FAT 7 g
PROTEIN 1 g
ENERGY 82 kcal/337 kJ

1 Crush the cardamom pods using a pestle and mortar or use the end of a rolling pin. Peel away the green outer casing then grind the black seeds. Mix the ground seeds into the butter with the lime rind and a little pepper.

2 Spoon the butter into a line on a piece of nonstick baking paper or foil, wrap the paper around the butter and roll it into a log shape. Chill until needed.

3 Steam the carrots in a single layer in the top of a covered steamer for 10–12 minutes until just tender. Transfer to a warmed serving dish. Unwrap the butter and arrange slices over the carrots.

SESAME GREENS
with Black Bean Sauce

Preparation time 5 mins

Cooking time 5–7 mins

Serves 6

5 teaspoons sunflower oil

2 tablespoons sesame seeds

1 tablespoon soy sauce

400 g (13 oz) spring greens or a mix of spring greens and Brussels tops

1–2 garlic cloves, finely chopped

3 tablespoons black bean sauce

CARBOHYDRATE 4 g

FAT 5 g

PROTEIN 3 g

ENERGY 70 kcal/294 kJ

1 Heat 1 teaspoon of the oil in a large frying pan, add the seeds and cook for 2–3 minutes, stirring, until lightly browned. Take the pan off the heat, add the soy sauce and quickly cover the pan with a lid. When the seeds have stopped popping, stir, put the lid back on and leave to cool.

2 Trim the spring greens and discard the stems. Thickly slice the leaves and rinse with cold water.

3 Scoop the seeds out of the pan, wash and dry the pan then add the remaining oil and heat. Stir-fry the greens and garlic for 2–3 minutes until just tender. Stir in the black bean sauce and cook for 1 minute. Sprinkle with the toasted seeds and transfer to a serving dish.

TIP You could lower the carbs even further by tossing the cooked greens with 1 tablespoon soy sauce instead of the black bean sauce.

PURPLE SPROUTING BROCCOLI
with Avgolemono Sauce

Lightly steamed, tender stems of deep purple broccoli are bathed in a light, frothy, Greek-style sauce, which is made with hot stock rather than melted butter, so cutting down on calories but not on flavour. It's also delicious served with steamed asparagus.

Preparation time 10 mins

Cooking time 10–12 mins

Serves 6

400 g (13 oz) purple sprouting broccoli

4 egg yolks

juice of 1 lemon

200 ml (7 fl oz) hot chicken or vegetable stock

salt and pepper

CARBOHYDRATE 2 g

FAT 5 g

PROTEIN 5 g

ENERGY 67 kcal/278 kJ

1 Arrange the broccoli in a single layer in the top of a steamer, cover and cook for 10–12 minutes until just tender.

2 Meanwhile, put the egg yolks and a little salt and pepper into a bowl set above simmering water. Use a handheld electric or balloon whisk to beat the yolks, then whisk in the lemon juice, a little at a time.

3 Gradually whisk in the hot stock and continue whisking until the sauce is thick and frothy. This should take 7–10 minutes in all.

4 Transfer the broccoli to a warmed serving dish. Serve the sauce separately in a warmed jug.

TIP This sauce must be made at the last minute for best results.

NEEP BREE
with Grated Ginger

This Scottish favourite is made with puréed swedes – known as neeps or yellow turnips by the Scots – chopped ginger and a little butter. Turnips contain much less carbohydrate than potatoes so are ideal for reducing your carb intake. They can be prepared in advance and reheated in the pan or in the microwave when needed.

Preparation time 15 mins
Cooking time 30–35 mins
Serves 6

25 g (1 oz) butter
1 onion, chopped
4 cm (1½ inch) piece of fresh root ginger, peeled and finely chopped
600 ml (1 pint) chicken or vegetable stock
1 swede, about 675 g (1lb 6 oz), cubed
4–6 tablespoons semi-skimmed milk
salt and pepper
chopped chives or parsley, to garnish

CARBOHYDRATE 8 g
FAT 4 g
PROTEIN 2 g
ENERGY 74 kcal/307 kJ

1 Heat the butter in a large saucepan until just melted. Add the onion and fry gently for 5 minutes, stirring constantly, until softened.

2 Stir in the ginger and stock. Add the swede and some salt and pepper and bring to the boil. Cover and simmer for 25–30 minutes until the swede is tender and almost all of the stock has been absorbed.

3 Purée in batches in a food processor or liquidizer, adding the milk as needed to make a soft purée.

4 Spoon the purée back into the saucepan and cover with a lid or transfer to an ovenproof serving dish and cover with clingfilm. Reheat when needed. Garnish with chopped herbs just before serving.

WATERCRESS SOUP
with Yogurt

This vibrant, bright green, creamy soup has a delicate peppery taste. Keep the GI rating and calories low by mixing it with yogurt instead of cream.

Preparation time 20 mins
Cooking time 14–16 mins
Serves 4

25 g (1 oz) butter
1 small onion, finely chopped
100 g (3½ oz) watercress, rinsed
2 tablespoons white long-grain rice
600 ml (1 pint) chicken or vegetable stock
300 ml (½ pint) semi-skimmed milk
150 g (5 oz) low-fat natural yogurt,
plus 4 tablespoons to garnish
salt and pepper

CARBOHYDRATE 18 g
FAT 8 g
PROTEIN 8 g
ENERGY 165 kcal/692 kJ

1 Heat the butter in a large saucepan, add the onion and fry gently for 5 minutes until softened.

2 Reserve a few sprigs of watercress for garnish and put them into a bowl of cold water. Tear the rest of the watercress into pieces and add to the onion together with the rice, stock and salt and pepper. Bring to the boil then reduce the heat, cover and simmer for 10 minutes until the rice is tender but the watercress is still bright green.

3 Transfer the mixture to a liquidizer or food processor and purée until smooth. Return to the saucepan, stir in the milk and yogurt and reheat gently for 2–3 minutes without boiling.

4 Ladle the soup into shallow soup bowls. Drop little dots of yogurt into each one using a teaspoon, then run a skewer through them to give a tear-drop effect. Garnish with the reserved watercress leaves.

TIP In summer, serve this soup chilled and add a few ice cubes as a garnish.

DU BARRY SOUP
with Parmesan Thins

This classic soup is made with puréed cauliflower, flavoured with nutmeg and mustard, and served with crisp shards of melted Parmesan instead of high-carb croutons.

Preparation time 25 mins

Cooking time 22–23 mins

Serves 6

1 tablespoon olive oil

25 g (1 oz) butter

1 onion, finely chopped

1 large cauliflower, cut into florets, woody core discarded

600 ml (1 pint) chicken or vegetable stock

450 ml (¾ pint) semi-skimmed milk

grated nutmeg

2 teaspoons Dijon mustard

salt and pepper

PARMESAN THINS

75 g (3 oz) Parmesan cheese, coarsely grated

paprika

GARNISH

150 ml (¼ pint) whipping cream

chopped chives

CARBOHYDRATE 10 g

FAT 22 g

PROTEIN 13 g

ENERGY 285 kcal/1183 kJ

1   Heat the oil and butter in a large saucepan, add the onion and fry gently for 5 minutes until softened but not browned.

2   Reserve a few cauliflower florets for garnish. Add the rest to the onion together with the stock and salt and pepper. Bring to the boil then reduce the heat, cover the pan and simmer for 10 minutes or until the cauliflower is tender.

3   Meanwhile, make the Parmesan thins. Divide the Parmesan into 24 loose piles on 2 large baking sheets lined with nonstick baking paper. Cook in a preheated oven, 190°C (375°F), Gas Mark 5, for 5 minutes until melted and just beginning to brown. Sprinkle with paprika and set aside to harden and cool.

4   Transfer the soup to a liquidizer or food processor and purée until smooth. Return the mixture to the saucepan. Stir in the milk, nutmeg and mustard and reheat gently for 2–3 minutes.

5   Cut the reserved cauliflower into tiny florets and dry-fry until lightly browned. Ladle the soup into bowls, swirl the cream into the centre of each, sprinkle with the fried cauliflower and chopped chives and broken pieces of Parmesan thins.

TIP This soup freezes well. To serve, add the cream and garnishes to the reheated mixture.

CRAB
and Ginger Bisque

Preparation time 40 mins

Cooking time 30 mins

Serves 4

1 fresh cooked crab, about 500 g (1 lb), cleaned and dressed

25 g (1 oz) butter

1 tablespoon olive oil

1 onion, finely chopped

1 small carrot, diced

2 tomatoes, skinned and diced

5 cm (2 inch) piece of fresh root ginger, peeled and finely chopped

150 ml (¼ pint) dry white wine

450 ml (¾ pint) fish stock

150 ml (¼ pint) semi-skimmed milk

salt and pepper

GARNISH

6 tablespoons double cream

paprika

CARBOHYDRATE 9 g

FAT 32 g

PROTEIN 8 g

ENERGY 373 kcal/1546 kJ

1 Keep the brown crab meat separate from the white meat that comes from the claws.

2 Heat the butter and oil in a saucepan, add the onion and fry gently for 5 minutes until softened but not browned. Add the carrot, tomatoes and half the ginger and fry for a further 5 minutes.

3 Stir in the wine, stock, brown crab meat and half of the white crab meat and season to taste. Bring the soup to the boil, cover and simmer for 15 minutes.

4 Purée the soup until smooth then return to the saucepan. Stir in the milk and remaining ginger and reheat. Ladle into bowls, swirl the cream over the top and sprinkle with the reserved white crab meat and a little paprika.

TIP If you have removed the meat from the crab yourself and think you may have left some pieces of shell in it, sieve the puréed soup to remove any odd bits.

MISO BROTH
with Prawns

This clear, hot, spicy Japanese soup is made with a base of miso, a fermented soya bean paste available from most health food shops, chilli, ginger, mirin and stock. Add diced tofu instead of prawns if you are serving this to a vegetarian.

Preparation time 10 mins

Cooking time 7–8 mins

Serves 6

4 spring onions or baby leeks, thinly sliced

2 cm (¾ inch) piece of fresh root ginger, finely chopped

½–1 large red chilli, deseeded and thinly sliced (to taste)

1.5 litres (2½ pints) fish or vegetable stock

3 tablespoons chilled miso

2 tablespoons mirin (Japanese cooking wine)

1 tablespoon soy sauce

100 g (3½ oz) pak choi, thinly sliced

2 tablespoons chopped coriander

150 g (5 oz) frozen cooked prawns, thawed and rinsed

CARBOHYDRATE 3 g

FAT 1 g

PROTEIN 8 g

ENERGY 57 kcal/240 kJ

1 Put the white parts of the spring onions or leeks into a saucepan with the ginger, sliced chilli and the stock. Stir in the miso, mirin and soy sauce, bring to the boil and simmer for 5 minutes.

2 Stir in the green parts of the spring onions or leeks, the pak choi, coriander and prawns and cook for 2–3 minutes or until the pak choi has just wilted. Ladle into bowls.

TIP Chillies vary enormously in intensity. If you are not sure how hot the type you have will taste, add half the amount and taste at the end of step 1. Increase the amounts as required. For greater heat, add the seeds.

LETTUCE WRAPPERS
with Crab and Cucumber Relish

Crab meat is given a Thai twist with a topping of raw cucumber relish flavoured with chilli, soy sauce and chopped mint before being encircled with crisp lettuce leaves. This unusual starter is great for a barbecue party.

Preparation time 30 mins

Cooking time none

Serves 4

1 fresh cooked crab, about 500 g (1 lb), cleaned

4 small iceberg lettuce leaves

salt and pepper

RELISH

¼ cucumber, finely diced

3 red spring onions, thinly sliced

½ large red chilli, deseeded and finely chopped

2 tablespoons white wine vinegar

1 teaspoon light soy sauce

1 teaspoon caster sugar

4 teaspoons finely chopped mint or coriander

CARBOHYDRATE 3g

FAT 2 g

PROTEIN 6 g

ENERGY 50 kcal/208 kJ

1 Make the relish. Mix all the ingredients in a bowl with a little salt and pepper.

2 Twist and remove the two large claws and spider-like legs from the crab and set aside. With the crab upside down, pull away the ball-like, spongy lungs. Check that the small sac and any green matter have been removed, then scoop the brown meat and skin from under the shell on to a plate. Break up the crab meat with a spoon.

3 Put the crab claws into a plastic bag, hit once or twice with a rolling pin to break the shells then, working on one at a time, peel away the shell, removing the white flesh with a small knife and a skewer. Add to the brown crab meat.

4 When you are ready to serve, spoon the crab into the lettuce leaves and top with spoonfuls of the cucumber relish, roll up and eat with your fingers.

TIP If you're short of time, use a ready-prepared and dressed crab or crab-flavoured white fish sticks.

CHILLI AND MELON SORBET
with Melon and Serrano Ham

This elegant and sophisticated starter is really easy to make. The sorbet can be prepared early in the day, or even days before, ready for quick assembly at the last minute.

Preparation time 35 mins, plus freezing

Cooking time none

Serves 6

1½ cantaloupe melons, quartered and deseeded

12 slices Serrano ham, Proscuitto crudo or Parma ham

SORBET

1 cantaloupe melon, halved, peeled and deseeded

2 tablespoons chopped mint

½–1 large red chilli, deseeded and finely chopped (to taste), plus strips of chilli to decorate

1 egg white

CARBOHYDRATE 7 g

FAT 6 g

PROTEIN 11 g

ENERGY 125 kcal/525 kJ

1 Make the sorbet. Scoop the melon flesh into a food processor or liquidizer and blend until smooth. Stir in the chopped mint and add chilli to taste.

2 Transfer the mixture to an ice cream maker and churn until thick. Alternatively, pour the mixture into a plastic box and freeze for 4 hours, beating once or twice to break up the ice crystals.

3 Mix in the egg white and continue churning until the sorbet is thick enough to scoop. If you are not serving it immediately, transfer the sorbet to a plastic box and store in the freezer. Otherwise, freeze for a minimum of 2 hours until firm.

4 Arrange the melon quarters and ham on 6 serving plates. Use warm spoons to scoop out the sorbet and put 2 spoonfuls of sorbet on top of each melon quater. Decorate with red chilli curls (see page 128) and serve immediately.

TIP If the sorbet is made a long while in advance, soften it at room temperature for 15 minutes or in a microwave in 15 second bursts on full power, until it is soft enough to shape.

SEARED SCALLOPS
with Lemon-dressed Lentils

Moist, golden-tinged scallops nestle on a bed of tiny Puy lentils, glistening in a lemon dressing and speckled with diced courgettes and leeks.

Preparation time 15 mins

Cooking time 21–22 mins

Serves 4

65 g (2½ oz) Puy lentils

150 g (5 oz) courgette, diced

75 g (3 oz) green leek top, thinly sliced

grated rind and juice of 1 lemon

3 tablespoons olive oil

3 tablespoons chopped parsley

12 small fresh scallops, rinsed in cold water and drained

salt and pepper

CARBOHYDRATE 13 g

FAT 10 g

PROTEIN 21 g

ENERGY 219 kcal/919 kJ

1 Rinse the lentils and put them into a saucepan. Cover with plenty of cold water, bring to the boil and simmer for 15 minutes until just tender. Add the courgette to the cooked lentils and cook for 2 minutes. Add the leeks and cook for 1 minute until just tender and still bright green.

2 Drain the lentils and vegetables into a sieve. Mix together half the lemon rind and juice, 2 tablespoons of the olive oil, the parsley and a little salt and pepper in the base of the pan, then stir in the strained lentil and vegetable mixture. Toss together to combine.

3 Heat the remaining oil in a nonstick frying pan, add the scallops and cook for 3–4 minutes, turning once or twice until browned and cooked through.

4 Spoon the lentils on to individual serving plates, arrange the scallops on top and sprinkle with the remaining lemon rind and juice and a little pepper. Serve immediately.

TIP The lentil mixture could be topped with thin strips of grilled salmon instead of the scallops.

GINGER SCALLOPS
with Asparagus

Preparation time 10 mins
Cooking time 10 mins
Serves 4

12 fresh scallops

2 spring onions, thinly sliced

finely grated rind of 1 lime

1 tablespoon ginger cordial

2 tablespoons extra virgin olive oil, plus
extra for drizzling

250 g (8 oz) thin asparagus spears

juice of ½ lime

mixed salad leaves

salt and pepper

sprigs of chervil, to garnish

CARBOHYDRATE 8 g
FAT 8 g
PROTEIN 37 g
ENERGY 248 kcal/1044 kJ

1 Wash the scallops and pat dry. Cut each one in half and place the pieces in a bowl.

2 Mix together the spring onions, lime rind, ginger cordial and half the oil. Season to taste and pour this dressing over the scallops. Set aside to marinate for 15 minutes.

3 Meanwhile, steam the asparagus spears for 5–8 minutes until tender. Toss them with the remaining oil and the lime juice. Season to taste and keep warm.

4 Heat a large, nonstick frying pan until hot, add the scallops and fry for 1 minute on each side, until golden and just cooked through. Add the marinade juices. Arrange the asparagus spears, salad leaves and chervil on plates with the scallops and any pan juices and serve.

TEA-INFUSED DUCK
with Flamed Pak Choi Salad

Marinating meat in tea is not as strange as it sounds. The tea adds a delicate, slightly perfumed flavour to the meat, which complements the warm salad perfectly.

Preparation time 25 mins, plus chilling

Cooking time 10 mins

Serves 6

3 teaspoons green tea (or 3 teabags)

250 ml (8 fl oz) boiling water

3 duck breasts, about 150 g (5 oz) each

3 tablespoons soy sauce

250 g (8 oz) carrots, cut into matchstick strips

4 small pak choi, about 400 g (13 oz) in total, leaves and stems thickly sliced but kept separate

3 spring onions, sliced

2 tablespoons orange liqueur

juice of 1 orange

CARBOHYDRATE 9 g

FAT 4 g

PROTEIN 18 g

ENERGY 148 kcal/620 kJ

1 Make the tea using the boiling water, leave to infuse for 5 minutes, then strain and cool.

2 Make crisscross cuts in the duck skin and put the duck, skin side up, in a shallow glass or china dish. Pour the tea over the duck breasts, cover with clingfilm and chill for 3–4 hours or overnight.

3 Put the duck breasts in a roasting tin, drizzle 1 tablespoon of the soy sauce over the skin and roast in a preheated oven, 220°C (425°F), Gas Mark 7, for 10 minutes until the skin is crispy but the meat is still slightly pink. After 5 minutes take 2 teaspoons of fat from the roasting tin and put it into a frying pan or wok. Reheat the fat, add the carrot sticks and stir-fry for 2 minutes.

4 Add the pak choi stems to the carrots and cook for 1 minute. Add the pak choi leaves, spring onions and the remaining soy sauce and cook for 30 seconds. Pour on the liqueur, light with a match and stand well back. When the flames subside, pour in the orange juice and warm through.

5 Spoon the vegetables into 6 small dishes and top with drained and thinly sliced duck breast.

CHICKEN TIKKA STICKS
with Fennel Raita

Marinate these tender cubes of chicken with yogurt, chilli, garlic and ginger earlier in the day or even the day before, then thread them on to skewers so that they are ready to grill. They are delicious served with the aniseed-flavoured raita.

Preparation time 20 mins
Marinating time 2 hours
Cooking time 8–10 mins
Serves 6

1 onion, finely chopped

½–1 large red or green chilli, deseeded and finely chopped (to taste)

2 cm (¾ inch) piece of fresh root ginger, finely chopped

2 garlic cloves, finely chopped

150 g (5 oz) low-fat natural yogurt

3 teaspoons mild curry paste

4 tablespoons chopped coriander

4 boneless, skinless chicken breasts, about 150 g (5 oz) each, cubed

shredded lettuce, to serve

FENNEL RAITA
1 small fennel bulb, about 200 g (7 oz)

200 g (7 oz) low-fat natural yogurt

3 tablespoons chopped coriander

salt and pepper

CARBOHYDRATE 8 g
FAT 5 g
PROTEIN 26 g
ENERGY 179 kcal/753 kJ

1 Mix the onion, chilli, ginger and garlic together in a shallow china dish. Add the yogurt, curry paste and chopped coriander and mix together.

2 Add the cubed chicken to the yogurt mixture, mix to coat, cover with clingfilm and chill for at least 2 hours.

3 Make the raita. Cut the core away from the fennel and finely chop the remainder, including any green tops. Mix the fennel with the yogurt and chopped coriander and season with salt and pepper. Spoon the raita into a serving dish, cover with clingfilm and chill until needed.

4 Thread the chicken on to 12 skewers and place them on a foil-lined grill rack. Cook under a preheated grill for 8–10 minutes, turning once, until browned and the chicken is cooked through. Transfer to serving plates lined with a little shredded lettuce and serve with spoonfuls of the raita.

TIP Soak wooden skewers in cold water for 30 minutes before you use them.

JAMBON PERSILLÉ
with White Burgundy Wine

This French terrine, one of the great specialities of Burgundy, where it is traditionally served at Easter, is made of strips of cooked ham set with a crystal-clear wine jelly speckled with parsley and tarragon. Serve in thick slices with salad.

Preparation time 30 mins, plus chilling

Cooking time 1½ hours

Serves 6–8

750 g (1½ lb) rolled smoked gammon joint, soaked overnight in cold water

1 carrot, sliced

1 onion, roughly chopped

2 bay leaves

½ teaspoon black peppercorns

200 ml (7 fl oz) dry white wine

150 ml (¼ pint) water

4 teaspoons powdered gelatine

2 teaspoons white wine vinegar

25 g (1 oz) chopped parsley

2 tablespoons chopped tarragon

4 spring onions, finely chopped

CARBOHYDRATE 4 g

FAT 10 g

PROTEIN 24 g

ENERGY 216 kcal/900 kJ

1 Drain the gammon and put it into an ovenproof casserole or pie dish with the carrot, onion, bay leaves and peppercorns.

2 Put the wine and water into a saucepan and bring to the boil. Pour this over the gammon, then cover the meat with a lid or foil and bake in a preheated oven, 180°C (350°F), Gas Mark 4, allowing 30 minutes for each 500 g (1 lb) plus 30 minutes.

3 When the gammon is cooked, sprinkle the gelatine over 4 tablespoons of cold water and leave to soak for 5 minutes.

4 Lift the gammon out of the dish and set aside. Strain the cooking liquid into a measuring jug, check the amount and pour into a saucepan. Boil for 5 minutes or until it has reduced by one-quarter. Take off the heat and add the gelatine, stirring until dissolved. Leave to cool.

5 Cut the string from the gammon and peel away the rind. Thinly slice the meat and cut each slice into strips. Mix the vinegar, herbs and spring onions into the gelatine mixture and pour a little into the base of a 1 kg (2 lb) nonstick loaf tin. Arrange a layer of ham strips, running along the length of the tin, to cover the base of the tin, add a little more jelly mix and continue layering until all the ingredients have been used.

6 Chill for 5 hours or until set. To turn out, dip into hot water, count to 10 then invert on to a chopping board. Remove the tin and cut into thick slices.

PEPPERED BEEF
with Horseradish-dressed Leaves

Hot peppery steak complements the cool salad beneath in an eye-catching yet light starter that is perfect to serve at any season. The quantities given here would also make a main course for two.

Preparation time 20 mins

Cooking time 3–5 mins

Serves 6

2 thick-cut sirloin steaks, about 500 g (1 lb) in total

3 teaspoons coloured peppercorns, coarsely crushed

coarse salt flakes

200 g (7 oz) low-fat natural yogurt

1–1½ teaspoons horseradish sauce (to taste)

1 garlic clove, crushed

150 g (5 oz) mixed green salad leaves

100 g (3½ oz) button mushrooms, sliced

1 red onion, thinly sliced

1 tablespoon olive oil

salt and pepper

CARBOHYDRATE 4 g

FAT 6 g

PROTEIN 19 g

ENERGY 148 kcal/620 kJ

1 Trim the fat from the steak and rub the meat with the crushed peppercorns and salt flakes.

2 Mix together the yogurt, horseradish sauce and garlic and season to taste with salt and pepper. Add the salad leaves, mushrooms and most of the red onion and toss gently.

3 Heat the oil in a frying pan, add the steaks and cook over a high heat for 2 minutes until browned. Turn over and cook for 2 minutes for medium rare, 3–4 minutes for medium or 5 minutes for well done.

4 Spoon the salad leaves into the centre of 6 serving plates. Thinly slice the steaks and arrange the pieces on top, then garnish with the remaining red onion.

RED PEPPER ROUILLE
with Saffron-roasted Mediterranean Vegetables

Rouille is traditionally served spooned over the top of Mediterranean fish soups such as bouillabaisse, but made with mild red peppers it also makes a delicious dip to enhance exotic saffron-marinated vegetables.

Preparation time 30 mins

Cooking time 30–35 mins

Serves 6

ROASTED VEGETABLES

4 tablespoons olive oil

2–3 garlic cloves, finely chopped

3 large pinches of saffron threads

3 mixed red and orange peppers, cored, deseeded and each cut into 6 strips

3 courgettes, about 200 g (7 oz) each

2 onions, cut into wedges

ROUILLE

250 g (8 oz) or 4 plum tomatoes

1 red pepper, cored, deseeded and quartered

1 garlic clove, finely chopped

large pinch of ground pimenton (smoked paprika)

1 tablespoon olive oil

salt and pepper

CARBOHYDRATE 14 g

FAT 10 g

PROTEIN 3 g

ENERGY 154 kcal/640 kJ

1 Put the oil for the vegetables in a large plastic bag with the garlic, saffron and salt and pepper. Add the vegetables, grip the top edge of the bag to seal and toss together. Set aside for at least 30 minutes.

2 Make the rouille. Put the tomatoes and red pepper into a small roasting tin. Sprinkle with the garlic, pimenton and salt and pepper then drizzle the oil over. Roast in a preheated oven, 220°C (425°F), Gas Mark 7, for 15 minutes.

3 Cool, then peel the skins from the tomatoes and pepper. Purée the flesh in a liquidizer or food processor with any juices from the roasting tin until smooth. Spoon into a serving bowl and set aside.

4 To serve, tip the saffron vegetables into a large roasting tin and cook in a preheated oven, 220°C (425°F), Gas Mark 7, for 15–20 minutes, turning once until browned. Spoon the vegetables on to individual plates and serve with spoonfuls of the rouille, reheated if necessary.

GRIDDLED ARTICHOKES AND FENNEL
with a Lemon and Caper Dressing

Preparation time 15 mins
Cooking time 7–8 mins
Serves 6

3 tablespoons olive oil

3 teaspoons finely chopped rosemary leaves

200 g (7 oz) fennel heads, stems separated and any large pieces halved

400 g (13 oz) can artichoke hearts, drained and halved

100 g (3½ oz) feta cheese, drained and crumbled

sprigs of rosemary, to garnish

DRESSING

grated rind and juice of 1 lemon

2 teaspoons capers, drained

4 teaspoons balsamic vinegar

salt and pepper

CARBOHYDRATE 3 g
FAT 9 g
PROTEIN 5 g
ENERGY 109 kcal/454 kJ

1 Put the oil, chopped rosemary and a little salt and pepper into a plastic bag. Add the fennel and artichoke hearts and shake gently in the bag.

2 Heat a ridged frying pan, add the dressed vegetables and cook for 3–4 minutes until the undersides are browned. Turn them over and cook for 2 minutes. Crumble the cheese over the top and place the pan under a preheated grill for 2 more minutes until the cheese is hot but not melted.

3 Meanwhile, mix the dressing ingredients together with any remaining oil in the plastic bag.

4 Spoon the vegetables on to serving plates and drizzle the dressing over the top. Garnish with extra rosemary leaves torn from the stems.

BLOODY MARY JELLIES
with Miniature Salad Garnish

All the flavour of a true Bloody Mary cocktail is captured in these dainty savoury moulds. Their small, elegant shapes conceal a mighty alcoholic punch.

Preparation time 20 mins, plus chilling

Cooking time 4–5 mins

Serves 6

3 tablespoons water

3 teaspoons powdered gelatine

½ cucumber

½ red pepper, cored and deseeded

¼ red onion

1 celery stick, with leaves

1 tomato

400 ml (14 fl oz) tomato juice

3 tablespoons vodka

8 teaspoons Worcestershire sauce

Tabasco or chilli sauce, to taste

salt and pepper

CARBOHYDRATE 5 g

FAT 0 g

PROTEIN 2 g

ENERGY 44 kcal/187 kJ

1 Put the water into a small, heatproof bowl and sprinkle the gelatine over the top, making sure that all the dry powder is absorbed. Set aside for 5 minutes.

2 Cut off a slice, 2.5 cm (1 inch) thick, from the cucumber and reserve. Pare away half the rind from the remaining cucumber and discard. Roughly chop the flesh and purée with the red pepper and two-thirds of the red onion in a liquidizer or food processor until smooth.

3 Finely dice the cucumber slice, the remaining red onion, celery stick and leaves and tomato and reserve for garnish.

4 Stand the bowl of gelatine in a small saucepan, half-filled with water, and simmer for 4–5 minutes until the gelatine has dissolved.

5 Mix the puréed vegetables with the tomato juice, vodka and 4 teaspoons of the Worcestershire sauce. Mix in Tabasco or chilli sauce and salt and pepper to taste. Gradually mix in the dissolved gelatine in a thin, steady trickle. Pour the tomato mixture into 6 small moulds and chill for 4 hours or until set.

6 To serve, dip each mould into hot water, count to 5, then loosen the top and invert on to a serving plate. Holding the mould and plate jerk to release, then lift off the mould. Spoon the finely diced vegetables around the moulds and drizzle with the remaining Worcestershire sauce.

Majestic
Mains

SEARED SALMON
with Vietnamese Salad

Crisp, crunchy carrot sticks and fresh-tasting Chinese leaves tossed in a dressing of rice vinegar, soy sauce and Thai fish sauce, topped with moist grilled salmon make an ideal dish for an informal supper party.

Preparation time 25 mins

Cooking time 8–10 mins

Serves 6

6 salmon fillets, about 150 g (5 oz) each

3 tablespoons chopped coriander

sprigs of coriander, to garnish

DRESSING

4 tablespoons sunflower oil

2 tablespoons rice vinegar

3 tablespoons light soy sauce

3 teaspoons Thai fish sauce

SALAD

250 g (8 oz) carrot, cut into matchstick strips

4 spring onions, cut into matchstick strips

400 g (13 oz) Chinese leaves, trimmed and sliced

100 g (3½ oz) bean sprouts, rinsed in cold water and drained

2 tablespoons chopped mint

50 g (2 oz) salted peanuts, chopped (optional)

Carbohydrate 8 g

FAT 30 g

PROTEIN 34 g

ENERGY 436 kcal/1810 kJ

1 Rinse the salmon in cold water and drain. Scatter with the torn coriander leaves and arrange on a foil-lined grill rack.

2 Make the dressing. Mix the ingredients together and brush a little over the fish slices. Chill the fish until ready to cook.

3 Make the salad. Mix all the ingredients together and chill until ready to serve.

4 Cook the salmon under a preheated grill for 8–10 minutes, turning the slices until they are browned and flake when pressed with a knife. Stir the dressing and toss with the salad. Spoon on to plates and top with the slices of salmon.

GRILLED SALMON
with Leek and Pancetta Confetti

This is a great main course to make when time is short. It takes minimal preparation and washing up and just 10 minutes to cook.

Preparation time 15 mins

Cooking time 8–10 mins

Serves 6

6 salmon fillets, about 150 g (5 oz) each

1 tablespoon olive oil (or oil from the tomatoes)

375 g (12 oz) pancetta, diced

625 g (1¼ lb) leeks, thinly sliced and rinsed in cold water

125 g (4 oz) sun-blushed or sun-dried tomatoes in oil, drained and sliced

small bunch of basil, torn into pieces

salt and pepper

1 lemon, cut into 6 wedges, to garnish

CARBOHYDRATE 4 g

FAT 41 g

PROTEIN 40 g

ENERGY 550 kcal/2285 kJ

1 Rinse the salmon fillets in cold water, drain and arrange on a foil-lined grill rack. Brush with oil and season lightly.

2 Cook the salmon under a hot grill for 5 minutes until browned on top, turn and cook for 3–4 minutes until the fillets are cooked through and flake when pressed with a knife and the flakes are the same colour throughout.

3 Meanwhile, dry-fry the pancetta in a large, nonstick frying pan over medium heat until the fat begins to run. Increase the heat and fry, stirring, until pale golden.

4 Add the leeks and stir-fry for 3–4 minutes until softened. Mix in the tomatoes and half the basil leaves, season to taste with salt and pepper and warm through.

5 Spoon the leek confetti on to serving plates and arrange the fish fillets on top. Garnish with the remaining basil leaves and serve with lemon wedges to squeeze over the salmon.

TIP Grilled, boneless chicken breasts or lamb chops could also be served in this way.

MONKFISH AND PRAWN FIRE POT
with Asian Spices

Not many people have a Mongolian table-top fire pot – a unique pot set over a small brazier with a chimney, which allows guests to cook their chosen ingredients in a richly flavoured stock. Use a covered saucepan or a large fondue pot and burner instead.

Preparation time 20 mins

Cooking time 11–12 mins

Serves 6

1 litre (1¾ pints) fish stock

4 teaspoons Thai fish sauce

3 tablespoons light soy sauce

2.5 cm (1 inch) piece of fresh root ginger, finely chopped

1–2 red chillies, deseeded and finely chopped (to taste)

2 lemon grass stems, finely chopped

5–6 kaffir lime leaves

4 shallots, thinly sliced

225 g (7½ oz) can mixed bamboo shoots and water chestnuts in water, drained

700 g (1 lb 7oz) monkfish, skinned, boned and cubed

400 g (13 oz) raw tiger prawns, peeled, deveined and rinsed in cold water

50 g (2 oz) sugar snap peas, each cut into 3

small bunch of coriander, roughly chopped

CARBOHYDRATE 6 g

FAT 1 g

PROTEIN 32 g

ENERGY 163 kcal/692 kJ

1 Put the first 8 ingredients into a saucepan. Bring to the boil, cover the pan and simmer for 5 minutes. Take the pan off the heat and set the stock aside until you are almost ready to serve.

2 Reheat the stock if needed. Slice the water chestnuts and add them, the bamboo shoots and the monkfish to the stock and cook for 2 minutes. Add the prawns and sugar snap peas and cook for 4–5 minutes until the prawns are bright pink.

3 Stir in the coriander leaves, ladle into bowls and serve immediately.

TIP Make sure the lemon grass is finely chopped because it can taste woody.

ZARZUELA
with Mussels, Calamari and Cod

Large chunks of white fish, mussels on their shells and rings of calamari combine to make this Spanish speciality (the name means operetta or musical comedy), which is richly flavoured with saffron and fresh tomatoes and white wine.

Preparation time 30 mins
Cooking time 24 mins
Serves 4

1 tablespoon olive oil
1 large onion, finely chopped
2 garlic cloves, finely chopped
½ teaspoon pimenton (smoked paprika)
500 g (1 lb) tomatoes, skinned and chopped
1 red pepper, cored, deseeded and diced
200 ml (7 fl oz) fish stock
150 ml (¼ pint) dry white wine
2 large pinches of saffron threads
4 small bay leaves
500 g (1 lb) fresh mussels, soaked in cold water
200 g (7 oz) cleaned calamari, rinsed in cold water
375 g (12 oz) cod loin, skinned
salt and pepper

CARBOHYDRATE 11 g
FAT 5 g
PROTEIN 32 g
ENERGY 240 kcal/1009 kJ

1 Heat the oil in a large saucepan, add the onion and fry for 5 minutes until softened and just beginning to brown. Stir in the garlic and pimenton and cook for 1 minute.

2 Mix in the tomatoes, red pepper, fish stock, wine and saffron. Add the bay leaves, season to taste with salt and pepper and bring to the boil. Cover and simmer gently for 10 minutes. Set aside until needed.

3 Discard any mussels that are open or cracked. Scrub the shells with a nailbrush, remove any barnacles and pull off the hairy tuft-like beard. Return the mussels to a bowl of clean water. Separate the calamari tubes from the tentacles and slice the tubes. Cut the cod into cubes.

4 Reheat the tomato sauce if necessary, add the cod and the calamari slices and cook for 2 minutes. Add the mussels, cover and cook for 4 minutes. Add the calamari tentacles and cook for 2 minutes until cooked through and all the mussels have opened. Gently stir and spoon into bowls to serve.

GRILLED SEA BASS
with Tomato Sauce

Preparation time 15 mins

Cooking time 12–13 mins

Serves 6

1 tablespoon olive oil

1 onion, finely chopped

300 g (10 oz) cherry tomatoes, halved

2 large pinches of saffron threads (optional)

150 ml (¼ pint) dry white wine

125 ml (4 fl oz) fish stock

grated rind of 1 lemon, the rest halved and thinly sliced

12 small sea bass fillets, about 100 g (3½ oz) each, rinsed in cold water

1 teaspoon fennel seeds

salt and pepper

basil or oregano leaves, to garnish (optional)

CARBOHYDRATE 4 g

FAT 7 g

PROTEIN 39 g

ENERGY 252 kcal/1057 kJ

1 Heat the oil in a frying pan, add the onion and fry for 5 minutes until softened and lightly browned. Add the tomatoes, saffron, wine and stock and stir in the lemon rind and a little salt and pepper. Bring to the boil and cook for 2 minutes.

2 Pour the mixture into the base of a foil-lined grill pan, add the lemon slices and set aside until ready to complete.

3 Arrange the fish fillets, skin side uppermost, on top of the tomatoes. Use a teaspoon to scoop some of the saffron juices over the skin, then sprinkle with salt and pepper and the fennel seeds.

4 Cook under a preheated grill for 5–6 minutes until the skin is crispy and the fish flakes easily when pressed with a knife. Transfer to serving plates and sprinkle with basil or oregano leaves, if liked.

BAKED TROUT AND PROSCIUTTO CROWNS
with Watercress Beurre Blanc

This light main course can be prepared in advance and cooked when your guests arrive. Use sorrel or rocket in the sauce instead of watercress if you prefer.

Preparation time 25 mins

Cooking time 20 mins

Serves 4

6 trout fillets, total weight about 875 g (1¾ lb)

juice of 1 lemon

6 slices prosciutto or Parma ham, about 75 g (3 oz) in total

150 ml (¼ pint) fish stock

1 teaspoon Dijon mustard

75 g (3 oz) butter, diced

2 tablespoons chopped chives

40 g (1½ oz) watercress, finely chopped, plus extra to garnish

salt and pepper

CARBOHYDRATE 0 g

FAT 29 g

PROTEIN 46 g

ENERGY 444 kcal/1853 kJ

1   Rinse the trout fillets in cold water, drain and place, skinned side up, on a chopping board. Drizzle with half the lemon juice and season with salt and pepper. Lay the ham slices on top, cut each fish fillet in half lengthways and roll up from the thicker end.

2   Put the trout in a shallow, ovenproof dish so that the cut edges are downwards. Pour the stock into the base of the dish and cover with foil.

3   Bake the trout in a preheated oven, 180°C (350°F), Gas Mark 4, for 15 minutes until they flake when pressed with a knife.

4   Carefully drain the fish stock into a small saucepan. Add the remaining lemon juice, the mustard and a little salt and pepper and boil for 3–4 minutes to reduce by about one-third. Gradually whisk in the butter, a cube at a time, to give a smooth, glossy sauce.

5   Arrange three trout crowns on each serving plate. Stir the chives and watercress into the sauce and spoon around the trout. Garnish with extra watercress sprigs.

TIP Add the chives and the watercress at the last minute because the lemon juice in the sauce will dull the vibrant green colour. For a richer sauce, use half stock and half dry white wine.

CREAMY LOBSTER
with Shallots and Vermouth

This luxurious and elegant dish is the perfect main course for a special celebration. For an intimate dinner for two, simply halve all the ingredients.

Preparation time 1 hour
Cooking time 10–11 mins
Serves 4

2 cooked lobsters, 625–750 g (1¼–1½ lb) each
2 tablespoons olive oil
2 shallots, finely chopped
4 canned anchovy fillets, drained and finely chopped
6 tablespoons dry vermouth
6 tablespoons reduced-fat crème fraîche
2–4 teaspoons fresh lemon juice (to taste)
pepper

GARNISH
paprika
rocket leaves

CARBOHYDRATE 4 g
FAT 15 g
PROTEIN 28 g
ENERGY 275 kcal/1158 kJ

1 Lay one of the lobsters on its back. Cut it in half, beginning at the head, down through the natural line between the claws, unfurling the tail as you cut downwards until the lobster can be separated into two halves. Repeat with the second lobster. Take out the black, thread-like intestine that runs down the tail and the small whitish sac (usually containing weed) found in the top part of the head. Leave the greenish liver as this is a great delicacy.

2 Twist off the big claws. Crack these open with poultry shears, a nutcracker, pestle or rolling pin. Carefully peel away the shell and lift out the firm, white meat, discarding the hard, white, oval membrane that lies in the centre of the claw. Twist off the small claws, taking care not to tear off any lobster meat from the body, and discard.

3 Scoop out the thick, white tail meat, slice and reserve it. Slowly and carefully remove all the remaining lobster meat from the body, picking it over for stray pieces of shell and bone. Rinse the shells and put them on 4 serving plates.

4 Heat the oil in a large frying pan, add the shallot and fry gently for 5 minutes until softened and just beginning to colour. Mix in the anchovies, vermouth and pepper and cook for 2 minutes.

5 Add the lobster meat and crème fraîche and heat through gently for no more than 3–4 minutes. Stir in lemon juice to taste. Spoon into the lobster shells and sprinkle with paprika and garnish with rocket.

SAUTÉED PRAWNS
with Tamarind and Lime

Delicately flavoured with dark, sticky tamarind paste, ginger and the fresh sharpness of lime juice, these jumbo prawns make a great centrepiece for an informal get-together. Provide a bowl for the debris, small finger bowls and a pile of paper napkins.

Preparation time 5 mins

Cooking time 10 mins

Serves 6

1 kg (2 lb) large, uncooked langoustine prawns in their shells (thawed if frozen)

2 tablespoons olive oil

1 large onion, chopped

3–4 garlic cloves, finely chopped

4 cm (1½ inch) piece of fresh root ginger, peeled and finely chopped

2 teaspoons tamarind paste

juice of 2 limes

300 ml (½ pint) fish stock

GARNISH

small bunch of coriander, torn into pieces

lime wedges

CARBOHYDRATE 5 g

FAT 5 g

PROTEIN 15 g

ENERGY 122 kcal/510 kJ

1 Rinse the prawns in cold water and drain well. Heat the oil in a large saucepan or wok, add the onion and fry for 5 minutes until just beginning to brown.

2 Stir in the garlic, ginger and tamarind paste, then mix in the lime juice and stock.

3 Bring the stock to the boil, add the prawns and cook, stirring, for 5 minutes until the prawns are bright pink. Spoon into bowls and serve garnished with torn coriander leaves and lime wedges.

TIP If you buy frozen prawns, make sure that they are thoroughly thawed in several changes of cold water before use.

THAI MUSSEL CURRY
with Ginger and Coconut Milk

A fresh-tasting, zingy mix of red chilli, lemon grass, shallot and ginger provides the base of this delicate coconut curry, which complements and brings out the flavour of the mussels without overpowering them.

Preparation time 30 mins

Cooking time 13 mins

Serves 4

½–1 large red chilli (to taste)

2 shallots, quartered

1 lemon grass stem

2.5 cm (1 inch) piece of fresh root ginger, peeled and chopped

1 tablespoon sunflower oil

400 ml (14 fl oz) can reduced-fat coconut milk

4–5 kaffir lime leaves

150 ml (¼ pint) fish stock

2 teaspoons Thai fish sauce

1.5 kg (3 lb) fresh mussels, soaked in cold water

small bunch of coriander, torn into pieces, to garnish

CARBOHYDRATE 6g

FAT 14 g

PROTEIN 21 g

ENERGY 230 kcal/967 kJ

1 Halve the chilli and keep the seeds for extra heat, if liked. Put the chilli, shallots and lemon grass into a liquidizer goblet with the ginger and process together until finely chopped.

2 Heat the oil in large, deep saucepan, add the finely chopped ingredients and fry over a medium heat for 5 minutes, stirring until softened. Add the coconut milk, lime leaves, fish stock and fish sauce and cook for 3 minutes. Set aside until ready to finish.

3 Meanwhile, pick over the mussels and discard any that are opened or have cracked shells. Scrub with a small nailbrush, remove any barnacles and pull off the small, hairy beards. Put them into a bowl of clean water and leave until ready to cook.

4 Reheat the coconut milk mixture. Drain the mussels, discarding any that are opened, and add to the mixture. Cover the pan with a lid and cook for about 5 minutes until the mussel shells have opened.

5 Spoon the mussels and the coconut sauce into bowls, discarding any mussels that have not opened. Garnish with torn coriander leaves.

TIP Chillies vary in intensity. This recipe includes a large, mild red chilli, but for extra heat choose one of the tiny but potent Thai red chillies.

BASQUE-STYLE CLAMS
with Hot Chorizo and Pimenton

This robust main course is flavoured with smoked sweet paprika and spiced chorizo sausage simmered in a garlicky fresh tomato sauce. Order the clams in advance from the fishmonger or use the same weight of mussels if preferred.

Preparation time 25 mins

Cooking time 15–17 mins

Serves 4

1.5 kg (3 lb) fresh clams, soaked in cold water

2 tablespoons olive oil

1 large onion, finely chopped

2–3 garlic cloves, finely chopped

¼ teaspoon ground pimenton (smoked paprika)

750 g (1½ lb) tomatoes, skinned and diced

400 ml (14 fl oz) fish stock

75 g (3 oz) sliced chorizo sausage, diced

salt and pepper

chopped parsley, to garnish

CARBOHYDRATE 12 g

FAT 13 g

PROTEIN 25 g

ENERGY 257 kcal/1083 kJ

1 Discard any clams that are open or that have broken shells. Scrub the shells with a nailbrush, remove any barnacles with a knife and pull off the small, hairy beards. Return the clams to a bowl of clean cold water.

2 Heat the oil in a large saucepan, add the onion and fry for 5 minutes until softened and lightly browned. Stir in the garlic and pimenton and cook for 1 minute.

3 Mix in the tomatoes, stock, chorizo and salt and pepper and simmer for 3–4 minutes.

4 Drain the clams and add them to the saucepan, cover and cook for 5–7 minutes until the shells have opened. Spoon the clams and the sauce into shallow bowls, discarding any clams that have not opened. Garnish with parsley and serve immediately.

DAUBE OF BEEF
with Mushrooms and Pancetta

This classic, slow-cooked, wine-infused beef dish is finished with buttery sautéed extras. It can be cooked up to the end of step 3 the day before, if preferred.

Preparation time 25 mins

Cooking time 3 hours 10 mins

Serves 6

3 tablespoons olive oil

1.25 kg (2½ lb) trimmed braising steak, cubed

1 large onion, chopped

3 garlic cloves, finely chopped

300 ml (½ pint) red wine

600 ml (1 pint) beef stock

1 tablespoon tomato purée

2 teaspoons Dijon mustard

1 fresh or dried bouquet garni

125 g (4 oz) diced pancetta or back bacon

300 g (10 oz) shallots, halved

4 large field mushrooms, wiped and sliced

salt and pepper

chopped herbs, to garnish

CARBOHYDRATE 8 g

FAT 19 g

PROTEIN 48 g

ENERGY 426 kcal/1780 kJ

1 Heat 2 tablespoons of the oil in a large frying pan, add the beef, a few pieces at a time, until all have been added. Fry over a high heat for about 5 minutes until browned. Lift out with a slotted spoon and transfer to a casserole.

2 Add the onion and garlic to the pan and fry for about 5 minutes until lightly browned.

3 Stir the wine, 450 ml (¾ pint) of the stock, the tomato purée, mustard, bouquet garni and salt and pepper into the onion mixture and bring to the boil. Pour the mixture over the beef and cover the casserole. Cook in a preheated oven, 160°C (325°F), Gas Mark 3, for 2½ hours until tender.

4 To finish, heat the remaining oil in a frying pan, add the pancetta and shallots and cook until lightly browned. Stir in the mushrooms and cook until golden then transfer to the casserole dish, adding the remaining stock, if needed. Cook for 30 minutes. Remove the bouquet garni and garnish with extra herbs and serve with steamed baby carrots and turnips.

TIP To make the sauce slightly thicker, boil it in a saucepan on the hob until it has reduced to the desired consistency. Do not thicken with flour as this will increase the carbs.

FILLET STEAK
with Roquefort and Walnut Sauce

Preparation time 10 mins

Cooking time 4 mins

Serves 4

25 g (1 oz) butter

4 fillet steaks, about 150 g (5 oz) each

ROQUEFORT AND WALNUT SAUCE

1 garlic clove, crushed

25 g (1 oz) parsley leaves, roughly chopped

15 g (½ oz) mint leaves, roughly chopped

1 tablespoon roughly chopped walnuts

75 ml (3 fl oz) extra virgin olive oil

2 tablespoons walnut oil

50 g (2 oz) Roquefort cheese, crumbled

15 g (½ oz) Parmesan cheese, grated

salt and pepper

CARBOHYDRATE less than 1 g

FAT 43 g

PROTEIN 37 g

ENERGY 540 kcal/2240 kJ

1 Make the sauce. Put the garlic, parsley, mint, walnuts and both oils in a food processor and process until fairly smooth.

2 Add the Roquefort and Parmesan, process again and season to taste with salt and pepper.

3 Melt the butter in a heavy-based frying pan. Season the steaks to taste and fry for 2 minutes each side for rare, or a little longer for medium rare. Transfer to plates, top with the cheese sauce and serve with cauliflower mash. Any remaining sauce, topped with a layer of oil, can be stored in a screw-top jar for up to 5 days.

MOROCCAN LAMB
with Cardamom and Ginger

Forget about plain rosemary and garlic-spiked lamb and try this Moroccan-inspired version with crushed cardamom pods, root ginger and garlic and a dry spice rub of cinnamon and paprika instead.

Preparation time 20 mins

Cooking time 2 hours 10 mins

Serves 6

2 kg (4 lb) leg of lamb

6 cardamom pods

2.5 cm (1 inch) piece of fresh root ginger, peeled and sliced

2 garlic cloves, sliced

1 tablespoon olive oil

ground cinnamon

paprika

bay leaves, plus extra to garnish

450 ml (¾ pint) lamb or vegetable stock or a mixture of stock and white wine

salt and pepper

CARBOHYDRATE 0 g

FAT 41 g

PROTEIN 57 g

ENERGY 594 kcal/2468 kJ

1 Use a small knife to make several slits in the lamb. Split the cardamom pods with a pestle or rolling pin and tuck the pods and seeds into some of the lamb slits. Tuck ginger and garlic slices into the others.

2 Put the lamb in a roasting tin, drizzle the oil over it and sprinkle lightly with the ground spices and a little salt and pepper. Tuck a few bay leaves under the joint then cover loosely with foil. Roast in a preheated oven, 190°C (375°F), Gas Mark 5, allowing 25 minutes for 500 g (1 lb) plus 25 minutes. Remove the foil for the last 25 minutes and baste with the meat juices once or twice during cooking. Add the bay leaf garnish to the tin for the last 5–10 minutes.

3 Transfer the lamb to a serving plate, keep hot and leave to stand while you make the gravy. Pour off all the fat from the roasting tin to leave about 3 tablespoons of the meat juices. Stir in the stock or stock and wine mixture, adjust the seasoning and bring to the boil, scraping up the bits from the base of the tin, and boil for 2 minutes.

4 Strain the gravy into a serving jug and garnish the lamb with the extra bay leaves. Carve and serve with slices of roasted butternut squash.

TIP Warn your guests about the whole cardamom pods and either get them to discard the pods or remove them while carving.

RACK OF LAMB
with Baba Ghanoush

Add some Middle Eastern flavour to roast lamb by cooking it with harissa (a hot spicy chilli paste) and a coarse lemony aubergine purée.

Preparation time 30 mins

Cooking time 57–67 mins

Serves 4

2 aubergines, about 300 g (10 oz) each

1 tablespoon olive oil

1 onion, chopped

2 garlic cloves, finely chopped

1 lemon, juice only

6 tablespoons chopped mint or coriander

2 racks of lamb, about 625 g (1¼ lb) each

2 teaspoons harissa paste

2 red peppers, cored, deseeded and quartered

200 g (7 oz) cherry tomatoes

250 ml (8 fl oz) lamb stock

150 ml (¼ pint) white wine

salt and pepper

CARBOHYDRATE 12g

FAT 80 g

PROTEIN 34 g

ENERGY 934 kcal/3860 kJ

1 Prick the aubergines and roast them, without oil, resting on the oven shelf in a preheated oven, 200°C (400°F), Gas Mark 6, for 30 minutes until the skins are blackened and the centre feels soft.

2 When the aubergines are cool enough to touch, peel off the skins and roughly chop the flesh. Heat the oil in a frying pan, add the onion and garlic and fry for 5 minutes until softened and lightly browned. Season and blend with the aubergine in a liquidizer or food processor to make a coarse purée. Stir in the lemon juice and herbs. Cover and set aside until needed.

3 Lay the racks of lamb, fat side up, in a large roasting tin, spread a thick layer of harissa over the fat and season with salt and pepper. Tuck the pepper quarters in and around the lamb.

4 Roast the lamb in a preheated oven, 200°C (400°F), Gas Mark 6, for 20 minutes for rare, 25 minutes for medium and 30 minutes for well done. Take the peppers out after 20 minutes and add the tomatoes for the last 5 minutes. Wrap the lamb in foil and set aside for 5 minutes.

5 Reheat the aubergine purée. Skin and slice the peppers. Drain all but 2 tablespoons of the meat juices from the lamb pan, add the stock, wine and a little salt and pepper and bring to the boil, scraping up the juices from the base of the pan. Boil for 2 minutes then strain into a jug. Spoon the aubergine mixture into the centre of 6 serving plates and top with the peppers. Cut between the lamb bones and arrange three cutlets on each plate. Arrange the tomatoes in a ring around the edge and drizzle with the sauce.

LAMBS' LIVER
with Campari and Orange

Liver is given an unusual twist here by adding a little Campari. Don't buy a bottle specially – you can use Grand Marnier, Cointreau, sherry or more orange juice instead.

Preparation time 10 mins
Cooking time 11–13 mins
Serves 6

500 g (1 lb) lambs' liver
2 oranges
2 tablespoons olive oil
2 onions, thinly sliced
4 tablespoons Campari
2 teaspoons Dijon mustard
2 teaspoons tomato purée
2 teaspoons clear honey
350 ml (12 fl oz) chicken stock
salt and pepper

CARBOHYDRATE 14 g
FAT 13 g
PROTEIN 18 g
ENERGY 248 kcal/1035 kJ

1 Rinse the liver in cold water, drain well and pat dry with kitchen paper. Grate the rind from the oranges or remove it with a zester. Peel the oranges and cut the orange segments between the membranes with a sharp knife.

2 Heat the oil in a frying pan, add the onions and fry for 5 minutes, stirring until pale golden. Push to one side of the pan (or remove altogether if the pan isn't big) and add the liver. Cook for 4–5 minutes, depending on the thickness of the liver, turning once, until browned.

3 Mix together the Campari, mustard, tomato purée, honey and stock and pour the mixture into the pan. Add the orange rind and segments and a little salt and pepper. Simmer for 2–3 minutes then serve with sweet potato mash.

TIP People either love or hate liver, so if you plan to serve it to guests, make sure you check beforehand that they will eat it.

VENISON MEDALLIONS
with Onion and Cranberry Confit

Full of gamey flavour, venison fillets are the most prized of all cuts and take just a matter of minutes to cook. Their rich flavour is complemented perfectly by the slightly sweet and tangy confit beneath.

Preparation time 15 mins
Cooking time 15–20 mins
Serves 4

25 g (1 oz) butter
1 tablespoon olive oil
4 venison fillets, 175 g (6 oz) each, cut from the saddle, tied at intervals with fine string
2 red onions, diced
150 ml (¼ pint) ruby port
2 teaspoons tomato purée
200 g (7 oz) frozen cranberries (no need to thaw)
4 teaspoons clear honey
salt and pepper

CARBOHYDRATE 23 g
FAT 11 g
PROTEIN 41 g
ENERGY 390 kcal/1643 kJ

1 Heat the butter and oil in a large frying pan, add the venison pieces and fry over a high heat for 5 minutes, turning until they are evenly browned.

2 Transfer the venison to a small roasting tin and roast in a preheated oven, 200°C (400°F), Gas Mark 6, for 10–12 minutes for rare to medium or 13–15 minutes for medium to well done.

3 Meanwhile, add the onions to the frying pan and cook for 5 minutes, stirring. Add the port, tomato purée and cranberries to the pan, cover and cook for a further 5 minutes until the cranberries have softened. Stir in the honey and salt and pepper.

4 Use a draining spoon to transfer the red onion mixture on to the centre of 4 serving plates. Thinly slice the venison and arrange in an overlapping line on top of Neep Bree (see page 49), if liked. Spoon the pan juices around the edge of the plates and serve with steamed asparagus tips.

TIP If using pork fillets instead of venison fillets, roast for 15 minutes in the oven.

POT-ROAST CHICKEN
with Tarragon and Lime

This rather homely, comforting dish has been given a modern twist by adding a dash of lime and serving it with spoonfuls of honeyed, herby crème fraîche.

Preparation time 20 mins
Cooking time 1¾ hours–2 hours
Serves 4

1.5 kg (3 lb) corn-fed chicken
1 lime
1 onion
1 carrot
200 ml (7 fl oz) dry white wine
600 ml (1 pint) chicken stock
small bunch of tarragon
375 g (12 oz) broccoli
300 g (10 oz) runner beans
bunch of spring onions
150 g (5 oz) reduced-fat crème fraîche
2 teaspoons clear honey
125 g (4 oz) sugar snap peas
salt and pepper

CARBOHYDRATE 17 g
FAT 41 g
PROTEIN 55 g
ENERGY 687 kcal/2859 kJ

1 Rinse the chicken inside and out with cold water then drain well. Grate the rind from the lime. Cut the lime into 4 quarters and put 2 into the body cavity of the chicken. Put the chicken, breast side down, in a flameproof casserole.

2 Cut both the onion and carrot into 4 and add the pieces to the casserole with the remaining lime quarters. Pour on the wine and stock then add 2–3 stems of tarragon and salt and pepper to taste. Bring to the boil. Cover and transfer to a preheated oven, 180°C (350°F), Gas Mark 4, for 1 hour.

3 Meanwhile, cut the broccoli into florets and the stems into slices. Trim and cut the beans into slices. Cut the spring onions into quarters. Mix the crème fraîche, lime rind and honey with a little salt and pepper. Chop enough tarragon to make about 2 tablespoons and mix into the crème fraîche mixture. Reserve the remainder for garnish.

4 Turn the chicken so that the breast is uppermost. Cook uncovered for 35–45 minutes until it is browned and cooked through. Remove from the casserole, transfer to a shallow serving dish and keep it hot.

5 Tip the chicken liquor into the base of a steamer and put all the broccoli and beans in the top. Cover and steam for 6 minutes. Add the sugar snap peas and spring onions and cook for 2–3 minutes until tender. Cut the chicken into portions, arrange in shallow soup-style dishes and spoon the vegetables and cooking liquor around. Pass the herby crème fraîche around and spoon on to the chicken to serve. Garnish with the remaining tarragon leaves.

FLAMING CHICKEN NORMANDE
with Apple and Calavdos

Preparation time 15 minutes

Cooking time 12–13 minutes

Serves 4

1 tablespoon olive oil

4 chicken breasts, about 150 g (5 oz) each

200 g (7 oz) shallots, halved

1 garlic clove, finely chopped

1 apple, cored and diced

75 g (3 oz) button mushrooms, sliced

4 tablespoons Calvados or brandy

250 ml (8 fl oz) chicken stock

1 teaspoon Dijon mustard

small bunch of thyme

salt and pepper

CARBOHYDRATE 6 g

FAT 8 g

PROTEIN 34 g

ENERGY 263 kcal/1103 kJ

1 Heat the oil in a ridged frying pan, add the chicken breasts and shallots and cook for 4 minutes until the chicken is browned on the underside.

2 Turn the chicken over and add the garlic, apple and mushrooms. Fry for 6 minutes until the chicken is cooked through.

3 Spoon the Calvados over the chicken and, when it is bubbling, flame with a match and stand well back. When the flames subside, add the stock, mustard, thyme and salt and pepper and cook for 5 minutes.

4 Cut each chicken breast into four and arrange the slices on a bed of shallots, apple and mushrooms. Spoon the sauce around and sprinkle with a little extra thyme.

ROAST GUINEA FOWL
with Salsa Verde

Moist and full of flavour, guinea fowl makes a smarter alternative to everyday roast chicken. It is baked with a little of the Spanish-inspired fresh herb, caper and anchovy sauce under the skin and served drizzled with the remainder.

Preparation time 30 mins, plus standing

Cooking time 65 mins

Serves 6

2 oven-ready guinea fowl, about 1 kg (2 lb) each

200 g (7 oz) extra fine green beans

75 g (3 oz) baby red Swiss chard leaves

pepper

SALSA VERDE

50 g (2 oz) can anchovies in oil, drained and finely chopped

3 tablespoons chopped basil

3 tablespoons chopped parsley or chives

3 teaspoons capers, roughly chopped

2 teaspoons Dijon mustard

4 tablespoons olive oil

2 tablespoons white wine vinegar

CARBOHYDRATE 2 g

FAT 16 g

PROTEIN 33 g

ENERGY 282 kcal/1177 kJ

1 Make the salsa verde. Mix all the ingredients with a little pepper in a bowl.

2 Rinse the guinea fowl inside and out with cold water and drain well. Loosen the skin over one of the breasts by carefully inserting a small knife between the skin and flesh at the top of the breast. Remove the knife and slide a finger into the gap to enlarge the space, working down towards the other end of the breast. When you can reach no further, loosen the skin from the other end of the breast to meet in the middle. Repeat with second breast then do the same on the other bird.

3 Spoon a little of the salsa verde under the skin on both guinea fowl. Put them into a large roasting tin. Cover loosely with foil. Roast in a preheated oven, 190°C (375°F), Gas Mark 5, for 65 minutes, removing the foil for the last 10 minutes, until browned and the juices run clear when you insert a skewer through the thickest part of the leg into the breast.

4 Transfer the guinea fowl to a serving plate, cover with foil again and allow to stand for 10 minutes. Meanwhile, cook the beans in boiling water for 5 minutes. Drain, return to the pan and toss with a little of the salsa verde and the red Swiss chard. Spoon around the plate and serve with the sliced guinea fowl, drizzled with the remaining salsa verde.

TIP Don't season the guinea fowl with salt because the anchovies in the sauce are already salty.

ORIENTAL DUCK
with Roasted Squash Salad

Preparation time 10 mins

Cooking time 20 mins

Serves 2

250 g (8 oz) butternut squash, peeled, deseeded and diced

4 teaspoons olive oil

2 small duck breasts, about 200 g (7 oz) each

1 teaspoon Thai seven-spice seasoning

2 star anise

50 g (2 oz) frisée lettuce

1 tablespoon snipped chives and whole chives, to garnish

salt and pepper

SMOKE MIX

8 tablespoons Jasmine tea leaves

8 tablespoons soft brown sugar

8 tablespoons long-grain rice

DRESSING

2.5 cm (1 inch) piece of fresh root ginger, peeled and grated

1 tablespoon rice vinegar

pinch of dried chilli flakes

4 tablespoons sunflower oil

CARBOHYDRATE 11 g

FAT 38 g

PROTEIN 41 g

ENERGY 545 kcal/2274 kJ

1   Toss the squash with 3 teaspoons of the oil in a roasting tin. Season and roast in a preheated oven, 220°C (425°F), Gas Mark 7, for 20 minutes.

2   Meanwhile, make the dressing by mixing all the ingredients together. Set aside. Brush the duck breasts with olive oil and rub with 1 teaspoon salt and the seven-spice seasoning.

3   Line a wok with 1 or 2 sheets of foil, making sure the foil touches the base of the wok. Add the smoke mix and star anise and stir together, then place a trivet over the top. Put the duck breasts on the trivet, cover with a tight-fitting lid and smoke over medium heat for 12 minutes. Remove the wok from the heat and set aside, still covered, for a further 5 minutes.

4   Put the lettuce and chives into a serving bowl, add the squash and dressing and toss to mix. Slice the duck breasts, garnish with chives and serve with the salad.

BRAISED PHEASANT
with Exotic Mushrooms

Pheasant can be dry, but if you wrap it in bacon and cook it with stock the meat will be partly steamed. Finish the pan juices with a little Marsala and some exotic mushrooms.

Preparation time 15 mins

Cooking time 37–43 mins

Serves 4

2 oven-ready pheasants, about 500 g (1 lb) each

25 g (1 oz) butter

small bunch of fresh sage leaves or a little dried sage

4 rashers of back bacon, about 150 g (5 oz) in total

300 ml (½ pint) chicken stock

100 g (3½ oz) exotic mushrooms, large ones sliced

6 tablespoons Marsala

salt and pepper

CARBOHYDRATE 1 g

FAT 26 g

PROTEIN 58 g

ENERGY 499 kcal/2080 kJ

1 Rinse the pheasants inside and out with cold water and drain well. Spread them with the butter and cover with sage leaves or a light sprinkling of dried sage. Season lightly with salt and pepper. Wrap each pheasant with bacon and put them in a roasting tin.

2 Pour the stock into the base of the roasting tin and loosely cover the pheasants with foil. Roast in a preheated oven, 190°C (375°F), Gas Mark 5, for 35–40 minutes or until the meat juices run clear when you insert a skewer through the thickest part of the leg to the breast.

3 Transfer the pheasants to a warmed serving plate and keep them hot. Put the roasting tin on the hob, add the mushrooms and Marsala, adjust the seasoning to taste and simmer for 2–3 minutes until the mushrooms are cooked.

4 To serve cut the legs off the pheasants and cut the breasts off the bone. Allow a breast and leg joint for each person and serve garnished with the bacon, cut into thin strips, and the mushrooms and sauce spooned around.

TIP Warn your guests to watch out for the shot when eating pheasant.

SIZZLING TOFU
with Bitter Gingered Greens

Not sure about tofu? Then prepare to be converted with this attractive oriental-spiced stir-fry made with gourmet baby vegetables and exotic sprouting seeds.

Preparation time 15 mins
Marinating time 15 mins
Cooking time 10–13 mins
Serves 4

250 g (8 oz) chilled tofu, drained
4 teaspoons sesame oil
3 tablespoons soy sauce
3 tablespoons sesame seeds
4 teaspoons sunflower oil
4 cm (1½ inch) piece of fresh root ginger, peeled and finely chopped
2 garlic cloves, finely chopped
2 shallots, halved and thinly sliced
2 x 250 g (8 oz) packs exotic baby leaves and sprouts (including peanut sprouts, pak choi, Swiss chard and asparagus tips)
1 tablespoon rice vinegar

CARBOHYDRATE 6 g
FAT 12 g
PROTEIN 11 g
ENERGY 170 kcal/707 kJ

1 Cut the tofu into 8 slices and arrange them on a foil-lined grill rack. Make diagonal cuts over the tofu and sprinkle with 2 teaspoons sesame oil and half the soy sauce. Leave to soak for 15 minutes.

2 Dry-fry the sesame seeds in a wok or large, nonstick frying pan for 2–3 minutes until lightly browned. Take the pan off the heat, pour the tofu marinade over the top and quickly cover the pan. When the seeds have stopped spitting, stir and spoon the seeds into a dish.

3 Rinse the pan if necessary and heat the sunflower oil and the remaining sesame oil. Add the ginger, garlic and shallots and fry for 2 minutes. Meanwhile, cook the tofu under a hot grill for 4–5 minutes, turning once until browned and hot.

4 Add the baby vegetables to the shallots and stir-fry for 2–3 minutes until just wilted. Mix in the rice vinegar and remaining soy sauce. Spoon on to plates and top with the grilled tofu.

CHICORY GRATINÉE
with Walnuts and Blue Cheese

Chicory is seldom served except in salads, yet its crisp, pale green-tinged leaves taste delicious dressed in a creamy blue cheese sauce and baked in the oven.

Preparation time 15 mins

Cooking time 30 mins

Serves 4

300 g (10 oz) or 3 heads of chicory, quartered lengthways

1 tablespoon cornflour

300 ml (½ pint) whipping cream

150 ml (¼ pint) semi-skimmed milk

2 garlic cloves, finely chopped

50 g (2 oz) walnut pieces

150 g (5 oz) blue d'Auvergne or St Agur cheese, diced

salt and pepper

CARBOHYDRATE 12 g

FAT 50 g

PROTEIN 13 g

ENERGY 540 kcal/2235 kJ

1 Arrange the quartered chicory pieces top to tail in a single layer in a roasting tin or ovenproof dish.

2 Mix the cornflour with a little of the cream to make a smooth paste. Gradually mix in the rest of the cream, then stir in the milk and garlic. Season to taste with salt and pepper and pour over the chicory.

3 Sprinkle the chicory with the walnuts and cheese, loosely cover with foil and cook in a preheated oven, 200°C (400°F), Gas Mark 6, for 20 minutes. Remove the foil and cook the chicory for a further 10 minutes until browned. Spoon into shallow dishes and serve with a salad.

TIP If you have 4 small oval ovenproof dishes, you could bake this in individual portions.

VEGETABLE TEMPURA
with Gingered Dipping Sauce

Preparation time 20 mins

Cooking time 10 mins

Serves 4

DIPPING SAUCE

2.5 cm (1 inch) piece of fresh root ginger, peeled and grated

½–1 large red chilli, deseeded and finely chopped (to taste)

4 tablespoons soy sauce

2 tablespoons dry sherry or white wine

4 tablespoons vegetable stock

1 garlic clove, finely chopped

VEGETABLES

500 g (1 lb) broccoli, florets and stems sliced

150 g (5 oz) cup mushrooms, thinly sliced

150 g (5 oz) baby corn cobs

150 g (5 oz) mangetout

75 g (3 oz) baby red Swiss chard leaves

TEMPURA BATTER

1 egg

100 ml (3½ fl oz) iced water

50 g (2 oz) plain flour

40 g (1½ oz) cornflour

½ teaspoon baking powder

¼ teaspoon salt

sunflower oil for deep-frying

CARBOHYDRATE 26 g

FAT 12 g

PROTEIN 13 g

ENERGY 264 kcal/1105 kJ

1 Mix together all the dipping sauce ingredients and divide them among 4 small individual dishes.

2 Arrange all the vegetables in individual groups on a baking sheet.

3 Make the batter. Mix the egg and water in a bowl. Gradually whisk in the dry ingredients until smooth.

4 Half-fill a large saucepan with oil and heat to 190°C (375°F), or until a vegetable dipped into the batter bubbles as soon as it is added to the oil. When the oil is hot, drop a small handful of the vegetables into the batter. Lift out one at a time, draining the excess batter, lower into the oil and cook for 2–3 minutes until the batter is crisp. Remove with a slotted spoon, drain on kitchen paper and keep warm. Continue dipping and cooking until the vegetables are ready.

5 Divide the hot vegetables among the serving plates and add the small bowls of dipping sauce.

AUBERGINE AND ALMOND ROULADES
with Garlicky Tomato Sauce

Lightly fried slices of aubergine are wrapped around an onion, ground almond and Parmesan stuffing and baked with a rich cinnamon-spiced tomato sauce to create a dish that's full of Mediterranean flavours.

Preparation time 30 mins
Standing time 15 mins
Cooking time 50–55 mins
Serves 4

2 aubergines, about 300 g (10 oz) each
2–3 tablespoons olive oil
2 tablespoons flaked almonds (optional)
salt and pepper

STUFFING
2 tablespoons olive oil
2 onions, chopped
75 g (3 oz) ground almonds
100 g (3½ oz) Parmesan cheese, freshly grated

SAUCE
1 tablespoon olive oil
1 onion, chopped
2 garlic cloves, finely chopped
400 g (13 oz) can chopped tomatoes
150 ml (¼ pint) vegetable stock
pinch of ground cinnamon

CARBOHYDRATE 15 g
FAT 33 g
PROTEIN 17 g
ENERGY 423 kcal/1758 kJ

1 Trim the stalks off the aubergines and cut them into long, thin slices. Arrange them in a single layer on a large baking sheet and sprinkle with salt. Leave for 15 minutes.

2 Rinse the aubergine slices in cold water, drain well and pat dry with kitchen paper. Heat a little of the oil in a large frying pan and fry the aubergine slices in batches, adding more oil as needed, until the aubergine is golden on both sides. Drain and return to the baking sheet.

3 Make the stuffing. Heat the oil in the frying pan, add the onions and fry for 5 minutes until lightly browned. Mix in the ground almonds and three-quarters of the Parmesan and season with salt and pepper. Divide the stuffing among the aubergine slices, roll them up and place in a shallow ovenproof dish with the joins underneath.

4 Make the sauce. Heat the oil in a saucepan, add the onion and fry for 5 minutes until lightly browned. Stir in the garlic, tomatoes, stock and cinnamon and season to taste. Simmer for 5 minutes then pour over the aubergines. Sprinkle with the reserved Parmesan and bake in a preheated oven, 190°C (375°F), Gas Mark 5, for 35–40 minutes until piping hot. Scatter the flaked almonds, if using, over the dish after it has been cooking for 20 minutes. Spoon on to plates and serve immediately.

WILD MUSHROOM STROGANOFF
with Vodka

Traditionally made with steak, this vegetarian stroganoff uses cup and exotic wild mushrooms flamed in vodka then simmered with stock and topped with crème fraîche.

Preparation time 15 mins
Cooking time 15–16 mins
Serves 4

25 g (1 oz) butter
1 tablespoon olive oil
1 onion, sliced
400 g (13 oz) chestnut cup mushrooms, sliced
2 garlic cloves, finely chopped
2 teaspoons paprika, plus extra to garnish
6 tablespoons vodka
400 ml (14 fl oz) vegetable stock
generous pinch of ground cinnamon
generous pinch of ground mace
150 g (5 oz) wild mushrooms, large ones sliced
6 tablespoons reduced-fat crème fraîche
salt and pepper
chopped parsley, to garnish

CARBOHYDRATE 6 g
FAT 13 g
PROTEIN 4 g
ENERGY 206 kcal/854 kJ

1 Heat the butter and oil in a frying pan, add the onion and fry for 5 minutes until lightly browned. Stir in the cup mushrooms and garlic and cook for 4 minutes. Stir in the paprika and cook for 1 minute.

2 Pour in the vodka. When it is bubbling, flame with a match and stand well back. Once the flames have subsided, stir in the stock, the remaining spices and season with salt and pepper. Simmer for 3–4 minutes.

3 Add the wild mushrooms and cook for 2 minutes. Stir in 2 tablespoons of the crème fraîche. Spoon the stroganoff on to serving plates and top with spoonfuls of the remaining crème fraîche, a sprinkling of paprika and a little chopped parsley. Serve with sweet potato mash.

TIP If you would prefer a thicker finished sauce, add a little cornflour mixed to a paste with water just before the end of cooking, but it will up the carbs.

BAKED CAMEMBERT SOUFFLÉ
with Cranberry Sauce

Impress your guests with this tall baked soufflé. Make the base and sauce in advance, then whisk and add the egg whites at the last minute once your guests have arrived.

Preparation time 30 mins

Cooking time 30–35 mins

Serves 4

65 g (2½ oz) butter

2 tablespoons grated Parmesan cheese

50 g (2 oz) plain flour

300 ml (½ pint) semi-skimmed milk

1 teaspoon Dijon mustard

4 large eggs, separated

175 g (6 oz) reduced-fat Camembert cheese, diced

salt and pepper

CRANBERRY SAUCE

175 g (6 oz) frozen cranberries (no need to thaw)

2 tablespoons water

2 tablespoons granulated sweetener

2 tablespoons balsamic vinegar

CARBOHYDRATE 16 g

FAT 33 g

PROTEIN 22 g

ENERGY 443 kcal/1843 kJ

1 Grease the base and sides of a 15 cm (6 inch) diameter, 9 cm (3½ inch) tall soufflé dish with some of the butter and coat this with the Parmesan. Use string to fasten a double strip of nonstick baking paper, 7.5 cm (3 inches) taller than the dish, around the outside.

2 Heat the remaining butter in a saucepan, stir in the flour, gradually mix in the milk and bring to the boil, stirring until thickened and smooth. Leave to cool for 10 minutes.

3 Stir the mustard and egg yolks into the sauce and season with salt and pepper. Mix in the Camembert and set aside.

4 Make the sauce. Cook the cranberries with the water in a small covered saucepan for 5 minutes until softened. Stir in the sweetener and vinegar and set aside until required.

5 Whisk the egg whites until stiff, moist peaks form. Fold a spoonful into the cooled Camembert sauce to loosen the mixture, then gently fold in the remainder. Spoon the mixture into the dish and bake in a preheated oven, 190°C (375°F), Gas Mark 5 for 30–35 minutes until the soufflé is well risen, the top is brown and there is a slight wobble in the centre. Remove the outer paper and serve immediately, with spoonfuls of reheated cranberry sauce.

VIETNAMESE VEGETABLE ROLLS
with Plum and Wasabi Sauce

These pancake rolls are low in carbs and calories and, unlike Chinese pancake rolls, are not deep-fried. They make a light main course for guests on a meat- and dairy-free diet.

Preparation time 30 mins

Cooking time 5 mins

Serves 4

200 g (7 oz) pak choi

2 tablespoons sunflower oil

100 g (3½ oz) sweet potato, cut into matchstick strips

100 g (3½ oz) carrot, cut into matchstick strips

½ bunch of spring onions, cut into matchstick strips

50 g (2 oz) bean sprouts, rinsed and drained

2 garlic cloves, finely chopped

2 cm (¾ inch) piece of fresh root ginger, peeled and finely chopped

50 g (2 oz) or 8 rice pancakes

bunch of coriander

SAUCE

4 ripe red plums, about 250 g (8 oz) in total

2 tablespoons water

1 tablespoon soy sauce

made-up wasabi (Japanese horseradish sauce), to taste

2 tablespoons granulated sweetener

CARBOHYDRATE 27 g

FAT 6 g

PROTEIN 4 g

ENERGY 176 kcal/734 kJ

1 Cut the leaves from the pak choi and slice the stems into thin matchstick strips. Heat 1 tablespoon of the oil in a wok or large frying pan, add the sweet potato and carrot and stir-fry for 2 minutes. Add the spring onions and pak choi stems and cook for 1 minute. Mix in the bean sprouts, garlic and ginger and cook for 1 minute. Transfer to a bowl.

2 Heat the remaining oil in the pan, add the pak choi leaves and cook for 2–3 minutes until just wilted.

3 Dip a rice pancake into a bowl of hot water and leave for 20–30 seconds until softened. Lift out and put on a tea towel, unfold one of the pak choi leaves and put it in the centre. Top with one-eighth of the vegetable mixture, keeping the matchstick strips facing as nearly as possible in the same direction. Add a couple of stems of coriander. Fold in the edges of the pancake, roll up tightly and arrange in a dish. Repeat to make 8 pancakes in all. Cover with clingfilm and set aside. Serve within 1 hour.

4 Meanwhile, make the sauce. Stone and chop the plums. Place in a small saucepan with the water, cover and cook for 5 minutes until softened. Purée the plums with the soy sauce then mix in the wasabi and sweetener to taste.

5 Arrange the pancakes on serving plates, garnish with the remaining sprigs of coriander and serve with small bowls of the sauce.

WARM GREEN BEAN AND ASPARAGUS SALAD
with Whole Eggs

A fresh summery lunch or supper dish made with a peppery nest of rocket leaves topped with a lightly cooked egg and surrounded with steamed green beans and asparagus with a black olive pesto dressing and topped with Parmesan shavings.

Preparation time 10 minutes

Cooking time 8 minutes

Serves 6

250 g (8 oz) fine green beans, trimmed

400 g (13 oz) fresh asparagus, trimmed

6 eggs

5 tablespoons olive oil

3 teaspoons black olive pesto

3 teaspoons balsamic vinegar

100 g (3½ oz) rocket leaves, rinsed

75 g (3 oz) stoned black olives

75 g (3 oz) Parmesan cheese, cut into shavings

salt and pepper

CARBOHYDRATE 3 g

FAT 23 g

PROTEIN 16 g

ENERGY 285 kcal/1180 kJ

1 Put the green beans into the top of a steamer, cover and cook for 3 minutes. Add the asparagus stems and cook for 5 minutes until the vegetables are just tender.

2 Meanwhile, put the eggs into a small saucepan, cover with cold water and bring to the boil. Simmer for 6 minutes until still soft in the centre.

3 Mix together the oil, pesto and vinegar in a small bowl with a little salt and pepper.

4 Arrange the rocket leaves in the centre of six serving plates. Drain and rinse the eggs with cold water. Drain again, gently peel away the shells and put one egg on each mound of rocket. Arrange the beans and asparagus around the edge then drizzle with the dressing. Add the olives and top with the Parmesan shavings. Serve immediately.

RED PEPPER TIMBALE
with Smooth Spinach Sauce

Deliciously moist, garlicky roasted vegetables are layered together and served with a vibrant dark green sauce.

Preparation time 35 mins, plus chilling
Soaking time 15 mins
Cooking time 45 mins
Serves 4

1 aubergine, about 300g (10 oz), thickly sliced
2 courgettes, about 400 g (13 oz) in total, thickly sliced
3 red peppers, cored, deseeded and cut into quarters
2 orange peppers, cored, deseeded and cut into quarters
4 tablespoons olive oil
3–4 garlic cloves, finely chopped
3 tablespoons balsamic vinegar
2 teaspoons ready-made pesto
50 g (2 oz) sun-dried tomatoes, drained
basil leaves, to garnish

SPINACH SAUCE
150 g (5 oz) young spinach leaves, rinsed and drained
3 tablespoons white wine
1 teaspoon clear honey
1 teaspoon balsamic vinegar

CARBOHYDRATE 17 g
FAT 21 g
PROTEIN 6 g
ENERGY 277 kcal/1152 kJ

1 Arrange the aubergine slices on a baking sheet and sprinkle with a little salt. Leave to soak for 15 minutes. Rinse, drain and pat dry with kitchen paper then return to the baking sheet.

2 Arrange the courgette slices and peppers, skin side up, in a single layer on a second baking sheet. Brush all the vegetables with the oil, sprinkle with the garlic, season with salt and pepper and roast in a preheated oven, 220°C (425°F), Gas Mark 7, for 10–15 minutes until browned.

3 Drizzle the balsamic vinegar over and cover the peppers with foil. Leave to cool. Peel the skins off the peppers with a small knife. Arrange the red peppers over the base and sides of a 20 cm (8 inch) spring-form tin. Cover with half the aubergine slices and dot with half the pesto. Add a layer of courgettes then the sun-dried tomatoes. Cover with the remaining aubergine slices, dot with the remaining pesto then complete with the orange peppers. Cover the vegetables with a small plate and weigh it down with a can. Chill for 1 hour or until needed.

4 Remove the plate and can from the timbale, loosely cover it with foil and reheat in a preheated oven, 190°C (375°C), Gas Mark 5, for 30 minutes.

5 Meanwhile, make the sauce. Cook the spinach in a covered saucepan for 2–3 minutes until just wilted. Purée with the wine, honey, vinegar and a little seasoning. Invert the timbale on a serving plate, remove the tin, garnish with basil leaves and serve, cut into wedges, with the spinach sauce.

Delightful
Desserts

CARDAMOM AND COCONUT SYLLABUB
with Almond Brittle

You can make the almond brittle a day or two in advance and keep it in an air-tight container until required. It makes a delicious crunchy contrast to the smooth coconut syllabub with its cardamom spicing.

Preparation time 15 mins, plus chilling

Cooking time about 10 mins

Serves 4

BRITTLE

50 g (2 oz) sugar

25 g (1 oz) flaked almonds, toasted

SYLLABUB

200 ml (7 fl oz) coconut cream

300 ml (½ pint) double cream

15 cardamom seeds, lightly crushed

2 tablespoons caster sugar

CARBOHYDRATE 19 g

FAT 57 g

PROTEIN 5 g

ENERGY 599 kcal/2478 kJ

1 Make the brittle. Put the sugar and almonds in a saucepan over a low heat. While the sugar melts, lightly oil a baking sheet. When the sugar has melted and turned golden, pour the mixture on to the baking sheet and set it aside to cool.

2 Pour the coconut cream and double cream into a large bowl. Add the crushed cardamom seeds and caster sugar, then whisk these ingredients together until lightly whipped and just holding soft peaks.

3 Spoon the syllabub into 4 glasses and chill. Meanwhile, lightly crack the brittle into irregular shards. When ready to serve, top the syllabub with the brittle.

RHUBARB AND GINGER PARFAIT
with a Spring Decoration

Pastel pink early rhubarb flavoured with root ginger is gently mixed with a rich custard, reduced-fat crème fraîche and whisked egg whites for a delicately light dessert. To enhance the feeling of spring, decorate with dark pink viola or pansy flowers.

Preparation time 20 mins, plus chilling

Cooking time 8–9 mins

Serves 6

400 g (13 oz) trimmed forced rhubarb

2.5 cm (1 inch) piece of fresh root ginger, peeled and finely chopped

5 tablespoons water

3 teaspoons powdered gelatine

4 egg yolks

6 tablespoons granulated sweetener

200 ml (7 fl oz) semi-skimmed milk

2 egg whites

125 g (4 oz) reduced-fat crème fraîche

few drops pink food colouring (optional)

pink viola or pansy flowers, to decorate

CARBOHYDRATE 5 g

FAT 7 g

PROTEIN 6 g

ENERGY 110 kcal/462 kJ

1 Slice the rhubarb and put the pieces in a saucepan with the ginger and 2 tablespoons of the water. Cover and simmer for 5 minutes until just tender and still bright pink. Mash or purée.

2 Put the remaining water in a small bowl and sprinkle over the gelatine, making sure that all the powder is absorbed by the water. Set aside to soak for 5 minutes.

3 Whisk the egg yolks and sweetener until just mixed. Pour the milk into a small saucepan and bring just to the boil. Gradually whisk the milk into the egg yolks then pour the mixture back into the saucepan. Slowly bring the custard almost to the boil, stirring continuously, until it coats the back of the spoon. Do not allow the custard to boil or the eggs will curdle.

4 Take the pan off the heat and stir in the gelatine until it has dissolved. Pour into a bowl, stir in the cooked rhubarb and leave to cool.

5 Whisk the egg whites until stiff, moist peaks form. Fold the crème fraîche and a few drops of colouring, if used, into the cooled custard then fold in the whisked whites. Spoon into 6 glasses and chill for 4 hours until lightly set. Decorate with flowers just before serving.

PETITES CRÉMETS
with Lavender and Strawberries

Preparation time 20 mins, plus chilling

Cooking time none

Serves 6

1 egg white

150 ml (¼ pint) double cream

150 g (5 oz) fromage frais

100 g (3½ oz) low-fat natural yogurt

4 teaspoons clear honey

2–3 lavender flowers, plus extra for decoration

400 g (13 oz) strawberries, hulled

CARBOHYDRATE 11 g

FAT 14 g

PROTEIN 4 g

ENERGY 185 kcal/768 kJ

1 Cut 6 squares of muslin, 18 cm (7 inches) square, and use them to line 6 ramekin dishes. Whip the egg white until stiffly peaking. Without washing the whisk, whip the cream until it is softly peaking.

2 Fold the fromage frais, yogurt and honey into the cream. Tear the flowers from the lavender stems and fold them into the cream mixture with the egg white.

3 Divide the mixture among the muslin-lined dishes. Bring the edges of the muslin together and tie them with string. Lift the muslin bundles out of the dishes and place them on a cooling rack set over a plate or baking sheet to catch the drips. Chill for 4 hours or overnight.

4 Mash the strawberries with a fork. Remove the muslin and string from the crémets and place each in the centre of a serving plate. Spoon the strawberries around and decorate with lavender flowers.

SEARED PINEAPPLE
with Hot Plum Sauce

Sweetened with natural sugars and just a light dusting of icing sugar, this fresh-tasting, eye-catching dessert can be quickly and simply put together when time is short. Serve with spoonfuls of reduced-fat crème fraîche or yogurt ice cream.

Preparation time 20 mins

Cooking time about 10 mins

Serves 6

500 g (1 lb) ripe red plums, stoned and diced

6 whole star anise

generous pinch of ground chilli powder and ground cinnamon (to taste)

8 tablespoons water

1 large pineapple, about 800 g (1 lb 10 oz) prepared weight, cored and sliced

2 tablespoons sifted icing sugar

CARBOHYDRATE 25 g

FAT 1 g

PROTEIN 0 g

ENERGY 102 kcal/435 kJ

1 Put the plums, star anise, ground chilli, cinnamon and water in a saucepan, cover and simmer for 5 minutes until softened.

2 Halve the pineapple slices and arrange them on a foil-lined grill rack. Dust with half the sifted icing sugar and cook under a preheated grill for 2–3 minutes on each side until lightly browned.

3 Arrange the pineapple on serving plates, spoon the hot plum sauce by the side and dust with a little extra sugar. Serve immediately.

TIP The riper the plums you use, the sweeter they will be. If you can find only under-ripe fruit, sweeten them with a little light cane sugar or sweetener.

COCONUT ICE CREAM
with Kaffir Lime

Preparation time 15 mins, plus cooling and freezing

Cooking time none

Serves 4

150 ml (¼ pint) water
75 g (3 oz) light cane sugar
6 dried kaffir lime leaves
finely grated rind of 1 lemon
400 ml (14 fl oz) can reduced-fat coconut milk
lemon or lime rind curls, to decorate

CARBOHYDRATE 23g
FAT 9 g
PROTEIN 1 g
ENERGY 168 kcal/705 kJ

1 Put the water in a small saucepan, add the cane sugar and gently bring to the boil, until the sugar has dissolved. Take off the heat, add the lime leaves, cover and leave to cool and infuse for at least 2 hours.

2 Remove the lime leaves from the syrup and reserve. Mix the syrup with the lemon rind and coconut milk.

3 If you have an ice cream maker, churn the mixture for 20–30 minutes until the ice cream is thick and spoonable. Serve immediately, or transfer to a plastic box and store in the freezer until required. Alternatively, pour the mixture into a plastic box, cover and freeze for 6–8 hours, beating two or three times with a fork to break up the ice crystals. Soften at room temperature for 15 minutes before serving.

4 Scoop into small glasses and decorate with soaked lime leaves and rind curls.

CHAMPAGNE GRANITA
with Wild Strawberries

Refreshing iced flakes of lightly sweetened champagne make an elegantly dainty dessert spooned into tall glasses and topped with tiny wild strawberries.

Preparation time 25 mins, plus freezing

Cooking time none

Serves 6

40 g (1½ oz) light cane sugar
150 ml (¼ pint) boiling water
375 ml (13 fl oz) medium dry champagne
150 g (5 oz) alpine or wild strawberries
few mint leaves, to decorate

CARBOHYDRATE 9 g
FAT 0 g
PROTEIN 0 g
ENERGY 80 kcal/337 kJ

1 Stir the sugar into the water until it has dissolved then leave to cool.

2 Mix together the sugar syrup and champagne. Pour it into a shallow, nonstick baking tin so that it is no more than 2.5 cm (1 inch) deep.

3 Freeze the mixture for 2 hours until it is mushy, then break up the ice crystals with a fork. Return the mixture to the freezer for 2 more hours, beating every 30 minutes until it has formed fine, icy flakes.

4 Spoon the granita into elegant glasses and top with the strawberries and a few mint leaves.

TIP The granita can be made the day before, but make sure that you mash it with a fork 30 minutes before serving to make it the right texture, then return it to the freezer.

MANGO SORBET
with Clementines

This refreshing and delicately flavoured sorbet is the perfect way to end a rich meal. When clementines are out of season, use 300 ml (½ pint) freshly squeezed orange or blood orange juice.

Preparation time 25 mins, plus freezing

Cooking time none

Serves 6

200 ml (7 fl oz) water

50 g (2 oz) light cane sugar

500 g (1 lb) clementines, about 7 in all, halved

2 large mangoes

1 egg white

grated rind and juice of 1 lime

CARBOHYDRATE 23 g

FAT 0 g

PROTEIN 2 g

ENERGY 95 kcal/404 kJ

1 Put the water in a small saucepan, add the cane sugar, bring gently to the boil and heat until the sugar has dissolved. Remove the pan from the heat and leave to cool.

2 Squeeze the juice from the clementines. Stone and peel one of the mangoes and purée the flesh until it is smooth. Stir the mango purée and clementine juice into the cooled sugar syrup and mix together.

3 If you have an ice cream maker, churn for 20–30 minutes until the sorbet is thick. Add the egg white and continue churning until it is well mixed and thick enough to scoop. Serve immediately, or transfer to a plastic box and store in the freezer until required. Alternatively, pour the mixture into a plastic box, cover and freeze for 2–3 hours until semi-frozen. Beat well with a fork or blitz in a food processor, then repeat the freezing and beating process. Mix in the egg white then freeze until solid.

4 To serve, slice the remaining mango and toss the slices in the lime juice and rind mixture. Take the sorbet out of the freezer and allow to soften at room temperature for 15 minutes. Scoop into dishes and serve with the mango slices.

MINTED ZABAGLIONE
with Blueberries

Preparation time 10 mins

Cooking time 7–8 mins

Serves 6

4 egg yolks

3 tablespoons light cane sugar

125 ml (4 fl oz) sweet white wine or sherry

150 g (5 oz) blueberries, plus extra to decorate

4 teaspoons chopped mint, plus extra to decorate

CARBOHYDRATE 10 g

FAT 3 g

PROTEIN 2 g

ENERGY 85 kcal/356 kJ

1 Put the egg yolks and sugar in a large bowl set over a saucepan of simmering water. Use a hand-held electric or balloon whisk to beat the yolks and sugar for 2–3 minutes until they are thick and pale.

2 Whisk in the white wine, little by little, then continue whisking for about 5 minutes until the mixture is light, thick and foaming.

3 Warm the blueberries in a small saucepan with 1 tablespoon of water and spoon them into the base of 6 small glass dishes. Whisk the mint into the foaming wine mixture and pour it over the blueberries. Stand the dishes on small plates or on a tray and arrange a few extra berries around them. Top with a little chopped mint and serve immediately.

FLOATING ISLANDS
with Blackberry Sauce

This classic French custard-based dessert is topped with poached meringues and served with a puréed blackberry sauce instead of the more usual – and more difficult – caramel sauce.

Preparation time 25 mins

Cooking time 11–14 mins

Serves 6

CUSTARD
6 egg yolks

3 tablespoons granulated sweetener

1 tablespoon cornflour

600 ml (1 pint) semi-skimmed milk

1 teaspoon vanilla essence

100 g (3½ oz) reduced-fat crème fraîche

MERINGUES
3 egg whites

2 tablespoons granulated sweetener

large pinch of ground cinnamon, plus extra for decoration

BLACKBERRY SAUCE
175 g (6 oz) fresh ripe blackberries

2 tablespoons water

CARBOHYDRATE 10 g

FAT 10 g

PROTEIN 9 g

ENERGY 157 kcal/656 kJ

1 Make the custard. Whisk together the egg yolks, sweetener and cornflour until smooth. Pour the milk into a saucepan, bring just to the boil and then gradually whisk it into the yolk mixture. Pour the mixture back into the saucepan and slowly bring almost to the boil, stirring continuously, until the custard coats the back of the spoon. Do not allow it to boil or the eggs will curdle. Pour the custard into a bowl, stir in the vanilla essence and leave to cool. Mix in the crème fraîche, cover with clingfilm and chill in the refrigerator.

2 Make the meringues. Whisk the egg whites until stiff, moist peaks form. Whisk in the sweetener a teaspoonful at a time, add the cinnamon then whisk for 1–2 minutes until thick and glossy. Half-fill a frying pan with water and heat to simmering point. Shape dessertspoonfuls of meringue into ovals by sliding from one spoon to a second and then into the water. Cook the meringues in batches for 3–4 minutes then lift out and drain well. Continue until all the mixture has been shaped and cooked.

3 Make the sauce. Cook the blackberries with the water for 5 minutes. Purée until smooth, then sieve if liked.

4 Pour the custard into 6 shallow dishes, arrange the meringues on top, sprinkle with a little extra cinnamon and drizzle the sauce around the edges of the dishes.

PIMM'S JELLIES
with Iced Lemonade

Capture the essence of English summertime with this light, fruity dessert, which is made without any added sugar. For special occasions, top with spoonfuls of reduced-fat crème fraîche or Greek yogurt.

Preparation time 20 mins, plus chilling

Cooking time 4–5 mins

Serves 6

3 tablespoons water

3 teaspoons powdered gelatine

1 apple, cored and diced

1 tablespoon lemon juice

250 g (8 oz) strawberries, hulled and sliced

1 peach, halved, stoned and diced

1 orange, peeled and cut into segments

150 ml (¼ pint) Pimm's No. 1

450 ml (¾ pint) diet lemonade, chilled

DECORATION

peach slices

strawberries, hulled and halved

mint sprigs or borage flowers

orange rind curls

CARBOHYDRATE 10 g

FAT 0 g

PROTEIN 2 g

ENERGY 85 kcal/357 kJ

1 Put the water into a small, heatproof bowl and sprinkle the gelatine over the top, making sure that all the powder is absorbed by the water. Leave to soak for 5 minutes. Stand the bowl in a small saucepan of gently simmering water so that the water comes halfway up the sides of the bowl. Heat for 4–5 minutes until the gelatine has dissolved and the liquid is clear.

2 Meanwhile, put the apple pieces in a bowl and toss with the lemon juice. Add the other fruits, mix together and divide among 6 glasses.

3 Stir the gelatine into the Pimm's and slowly mix in the lemonade. Pour over the fruit in the glasses then transfer to the refrigerator for at least 4 hours to chill and set.

4 To serve, decorate the tops of the glasses with peach slices, strawberry halves, sprigs of mint or borage flowers and orange rind curls.

TIP To make orange rind curls, use a canelle knife to pare the rind away from the fruit in strips, then wrap them tightly around a skewer or the handle of a wooden spoon. Slide them off after a minute or two and repeat to make as many curls as needed.

BITTER CHOCOLATE MOUSSE
with Chilli and Cinnamon

Following Aztec tradition, chocolate is mixed with a little chilli and cinnamon to bring out its full flavour. If you are unsure about the intensity of the chillies you are using, mix in the flavoured milk gradually and taste as you go.

Preparation time 15 mins, plus chilling

Cooking time 5 mins

Serves 6

1 large red chilli, deseeded and finely chopped

5 tablespoons semi-skimmed milk

175 g (6 oz) dark chocolate, broken into pieces

2 large pinches of ground cinnamon

15 g (½ oz) butter

3 eggs, separated

2 teaspoons granulated sweetener (optional)

DECORATION

6 tablespoons reduced-fat crème fraîche

red chilli curls

drinking chocolate

CARBOHYDRATE 23 g

FAT 17 g

PROTEIN 6 g

ENERGY 262 kcal/1093 kJ

1 Put the chopped chilli and milk in a small saucepan and bring just to the boil. Take off the heat and leave to infuse for 1 hour.

2 Put the chocolate in a bowl with the cinnamon and butter and set over a saucepan of just-boiled water, making sure that the base of the bowl does not touch the water. Set aside for 5 minutes or until the chocolate and butter have melted.

3 Take the bowl off the heat, stir in the egg yolks and sweetener, if using. Strain and reserve the chilli and gradually mix the milk into the chocolate, tasting as you go until you have the strength of chilli that you like. If you like spicy food, add a little of the chopped chilli too.

4 Whisk the egg whites until softly peaking. Fold a spoonful into the chocolate mixture to loosen it, then fold in the remainder. Pour into 6 small glass dishes and chill for 4 hours or until set.

5 Spoon the crème fraîche on top, add a few chilli curls and a light dusting of chocolate powder.

TIP To make the chilli curls, core and deseed a red chilli and cut it into thin strips. Put the strips into iced water and soak for 15–20 minutes until curled. Drain well before use. Wash your hands after touching chillies or use rubber gloves.

CHOCOLATE MOUSSE CAKE
with Amaretto Cream

Preparation time 30 mins

Cooking time 30–35 mins

Serves 8

250 g (8 oz) dark chocolate, broken
into pieces

125 g (4 oz) unsalted butter, diced

5 eggs, separated

3 tablespoons semi-skimmed milk

4 tablespoons granulated sweetener

1 teaspoon vanilla essence

sifted cocoa and chocolate curls, to decorate

AMARETTO CREAM

150 ml (¼ pint) whipping cream

100 g (3½ oz) fromage frais

2 tablespoons Amaretto liqueur

CARBOHYDRATE 24 g

FAT 34 g

PROTEIN 7 g

ENERGY 429 kcal/1782 kJ

1 Put the chocolate and butter in a saucepan and heat gently until melted. Meanwhile, line the base and sides of a 23 cm (9 inch) spring-form tin with nonstick baking paper. Take the chocolate pan off the heat and stir in the egg yolks, milk, sweetener and vanilla.

2 Whisk the egg whites until stiff, moist peaks form. Fold a tablespoon into the chocolate mixture to loosen it slightly then fold in the remainder.

3 Pour the mixture into the tin. Bake in a preheated oven, 180°C (350°F), Gas Mark 4, for 30–35 minutes until well risen and the centre is still slightly spongy. Leave to cool in the tin. (The cake sinks on cooling.)

4 Whip the cream and fold in the fromage frais and liqueur. Serve with a slice of cake dusted with a little sifted cocoa and sprinkled with chocolate curls.

COFFEE PANNA COTTA
with Coffee Liqueur and Chocolate

These velvety smooth, just-set Italian custard desserts melt in the mouth. Served with a drizzle of coffee liqueur they are the perfect finale for a special meal.

Preparation time 20 mins, plus chilling

Cooking time 3–4 mins

Serves 6

4 tablespoons water
4 teaspoons powdered gelatine
2 egg yolks
50 g (2 oz) light cane sugar
300 ml (½ pint) semi-skimmed milk
150 g (5 oz) reduced-fat mascarpone cheese
200 ml (7 fl oz) strong black coffee
1 teaspoon vanilla essence
6 teaspoons coffee liqueur

DECORATION
few chocolate curls
chocolate-covered coffee beans (optional)
sifted cocoa

CARBOHYDRATE 15 g
FAT 11 g
PROTEIN 5 g
ENERGY 180 kcal/762 kJ

1 Put the water in a small, heatproof bowl and sprinkle the gelatine over the top, making sure that the all the powder is absorbed by the water. Leave to soak for 5 minutes.

2 Whisk together the egg yolks and sugar in a bowl for a few minutes until light and thick. Pour the milk into a saucepan, bring just to the boil and gradually whisk into the egg yolk mixture. Pour the milk mixture back into the saucepan and heat gently for 3–4 minutes until the custard thinly coats the back of a wooden spoon. Do not allow the custard to boil or the eggs will separate.

3 Take the pan off the heat and add the gelatine. Stir until it has melted, add the mascarpone and stir until that has melted. Stir in the coffee and vanilla, pour into 6 small individual moulds and chill for 4 hours or until set. To serve, dip the moulds, one at a time, into a bowl of just-boiled water. Count to 5, invert the mould on a serving plate and tap to release.

4 Drizzle the coffee liqueur around the base of the plate and top the desserts with chocolate curls (made using a swivel vegetable peeler), chocolate-covered coffee beans, if using, and dust with cocoa.

TIP Before you pour the custard into the moulds, taste it and adjust the coffee strength, stirring in a little extra instant coffee, if necessary. There's no need to dissolve the coffee in water first because the custard mixture will still be warm.

BRÛLÉE VANILLA CHEESECAKE
with Oranges

If you thought cheesecake would be off the menu, think again. This reduced-fat version is made without the high-carb biscuit base and has sweetener instead of sugar to keep the carbs to the minimum.

Preparation time 30 mins, plus chilling

Cooking time 30–35 mins

Serves 6–8

3 x 200 g (7 oz) packets of low-fat soft cheese (1% fat)

6 tablespoons granulated sweetener

1½ teaspoons vanilla essence

finely grated rind of ½ orange

4 eggs, separated

1 tablespoon icing sugar, sifted

3 oranges, peeled and cut into segments

CARBOHYDRATE 14 g

FAT 4 g

PROTEIN 17 g

ENERGY 160 kcal/675 kJ

1 In a bowl, mix together the low-fat soft cheese, sweetener, vanilla essence, orange rind and egg yolks until smooth.

2 Whisk the egg whites until softly peaking, then fold a large spoonful into the cheese mixture to loosen it. Add the remaining egg whites and fold them in gently.

3 Pour the mixture into a buttered, 20 cm (8 inch) springform tin and level the surface. Bake in a preheated oven, 160°C (325°F), Gas Mark 3, for 30–35 minutes until well risen, golden brown and just set in the centre.

4 Turn off the oven and leave the cheesecake to cool for 15 minutes with the door slightly ajar. Take it out of the oven, leave to cool, then chill in the refrigerator for 4 hours. (The cheesecake sinks slightly as it cools.)

5 Run a knife around the cheesecake, loosen the tin and transfer to a serving plate. Dust the top with the sifted icing sugar and caramelize the sugar with a cook's blowtorch. Serve within 30 minutes, while the sugar topping is still hard and brittle. Cut into wedges and arrange on plates with the orange segments.

TIP If you don't have a cook's blowtorch, leave the icing sugar as it is.

ORCHARD FRUITS
with Muscat Wine and Bay Cream

Bay leaves are often used in savoury dishes, but here they add a light, delicate flavour that perfectly complements the wine and cream.

Preparation time 25 mins, plus chilling

Cooking time 5 7 mins

Serves 6

200 ml (7 fl oz) double cream

6 bay leaves

3 small pears

3 small sweet dessert apples

250 ml (8 fl oz) Muscat (sweet white) wine

pared rind, cut into thin strips, and juice of ½ orange

2 teaspoons clear honey

CARBOHYDRATE 16 g

FAT 16 g

PROTEIN 1 g

ENERGY 240 kcal/999 kJ

1 Pour the cream into a small saucepan, add three of the bay leaves and bring the cream just to the boil. Take off the heat, cool and chill for 2 hours.

2 Peel the pears and apples and cut them in half, cutting down through the stalks too. Carefully scoop the cores away with a small spoon or knife.

3 Put the fruits in a medium saucepan with the wine, the remaining bay leaves and orange rind. Cover and simmer for 5–10 minutes, depending on the firmness of the pears. Leave to cool.

4 Take the bay leaves out of the cream and discard them. Whip the cream until softly peaking then fold in the orange juice, honey and 3 tablespoons of the cooled wine from the fruit. Chill until needed.

5 Arrange the fruit in a glass dish and serve with spoonfuls of cream.

TIP Pare the rind from a whole orange before cutting and squeezing.

ICED BANANA AND YOGURT TORTE
with Pistachios and Passion Fruit

This exotic, Italian-inspired ice cream is moulded in a loaf tin then unmoulded and served, cut into slices, with extra passion fruit.

Preparation time 25 mins, plus freezing

Cooking time none

Serves 6

1 medium ripe banana, about 175 g (6 oz), with skin on

300 g (10 oz) low-fat natural yogurt

200 g (7 oz) reduced-fat mascarpone cheese

3 tablespoons granulated sweetener

2 passion fruit, halved

grated rind and juice of 1 lime

25 g (1 oz) pistachio nuts, roughly chopped, plus extra to decorate

2 egg whites

2 passion fruit, to decorate (optional)

CARBOHYDRATE 14 g

FAT 13 g

PROTEIN 7 g

ENERGY 196 kcal/827 kJ

1 Line a 1 kg (2 lb) loaf tin with clingfilm and chill in the freezer for 15 minutes.

2 Peel the banana and mash it with a fork. Mix it with the yogurt, mascarpone and sweetener until smooth. Scoop the seeds from the passion fruit into the yogurt mixture and stir in with the lime rind and juice and the nuts.

3 Whisk the egg whites until stiff, moist peaks form, then fold into the yogurt mixture. Spoon into the prepared tin and level the top. Freeze for 4 hours or overnight until firm.

4 Before serving, leave the torte to stand at room temperature for 10–20 minutes to soften slightly. Invert on to a chopping board, peel away the clingfilm and use a hot knife to cut thick slices. Transfer to serving plates, decorate with pistachio nuts and spoonfuls of the extra passion fruit seeds, if liked.

TEA CREAMS
with Prune Compote

This is a light, subtle dessert that makes a great talking point at a dinner party. There's no fussy whisking of eggs or cream – just stir cream and gelatine into milky Earl Grey tea, chill, then unmould and serve with tea-soaked prunes.

Preparation time 20 mins, plus chilling

Cooking time 2 mins

Serves 6

3 tablespoons cold water

3 teaspoons powdered gelatine

300 ml (½ pint) semi-skimmed milk

5 teaspoons Earl Grey tea leaves

300 ml (½ pint) boiling water

200 g (7 oz) ready-to-eat, dried, pitted prunes

3 tablespoons granulated sweetener

300 ml (½ pint) single cream

CARBOHYDRATE 17 g

FAT 11 g

PROTEIN 5 g

ENERGY 176 kcal/735 kJ

1 Put the cold water into a small bowl and sprinkle the gelatine over the top, making sure that all the powder is absorbed. Set aside to soak.

2 Pour the milk into a small saucepan, bring it just to the boil then take off the heat and add 3 teaspoons of the tea. Set aside for a few minutes to brew.

3 Strain the tea-infused milk and pour it back into the saucepan. Add the soaked gelatine and heat gently, stirring, until the gelatine has dissolved. Leave to cool.

4 Put the remaining tea into a warmed teapot, pour over the boiling water and leave to infuse for a few minutes. Put the prunes and 1 tablespoon of the sweetener into a bowl, strain the warm tea over the top and mix together.

5 Mix the cooled milk with the cream and the remaining sweetener. Pour into 6 small, individual moulds and chill for 4 hours or until set. Cover the prunes and leave at room temperature.

6 Dip each mould into a bowl of hot water, count to 5, loosen the edges and invert the moulds on to small serving plates. Remove the moulds and spoon the prunes on to the plates.

TIP If you don't have individual moulds, set the desserts in small wine glasses and when set top with diced soaked prunes.

TIPSY BLUEBERRY POTS
with Mascarpone

Mascarpone cheese adds a silky-smooth creaminess to this quick and easy dessert. Serve it in small, china pots or tall, elegant glasses. As an alternative, try a combination of blueberries, raspberries and strawberries or just strawberries on their own.

Preparation time 15 mins, plus soaking

Cooking time none

Serves 4

200 g (7 oz) blueberries
2 tablespoons kirsch or vodka
150 g (5 oz) reduced-fat mascarpone cheese
150 g (5 oz) low-fat natural yogurt
2 tablespoons granulated sweetener
grated rind and juice of 1 lime

CARBOHYDRATE 9 g

FAT 12 g

PROTEIN 5 g

ENERGY 175 kcal/734 kJ

1 Roughly mash 150 g (5 oz) of the blueberries with a fork, combine with the alcohol and leave to soak for at least 1 hour.

2 Beat together the mascarpone and yogurt until smooth then mix in the sweetener and the lime rind and juice.

3 Layer alternate spoonfuls of mashed blueberries and mascarpone into individual dishes. Top with the whole blueberries and chill until ready to serve.

GRILLED HONEY PEARS
with Minted Mascarpone Cream

Preparation time 10 mins

Cooking time 5 mins

Serves 4

30 g (1¼ oz) butter

2 tablespoons clear honey

4 ripe pears, such as Red William, cored and sliced lengthways

lemon juice

MINTED MASCARPONE CREAM

1 tablespoon finely chopped mint

1 tablespoon granulated sweetener

175 g (6 oz) reduced-fat mascarpone cheese

DECORATION

mint sprigs

icing sugar

ground cinnamon

CARBOHYDRATE 27g

FAT 19 g

PROTEIN 4 g

ENERGY 293 kcal/715 kJ

1 Melt the butter in a small saucepan. Remove from the heat and stir in the honey.

2 Sprinkle the pear slices with a little lemon juice as soon as they are prepared to prevent them from discolouring. Line a baking sheet with foil and lay the pear slices on it. Brush the pears with the butter and honey mixture. Preheat the grill to the hottest setting and grill the pears for 5 minutes.

3 Meanwhile, make the minted mascarpone cream by lightly whisking the chopped mint and the sweetener into the mascarpone.

4 Divide the pear slices among 4 plates and add a dollop of the minted mascarpone cream and mint sprig to each portion. Lightly dust with icing sugar and ground cinnamon and serve immediately.

RICOTTA, PLUM AND ALMOND CAKE
with Smooth Plum Sauce

This light, flour- and sugar-free cake will fool your dinner party guests – don't let them in on the secret until after they have tried it.

Preparation time 30 mins

Cooking time 40 mins

Serves 6

500 g (1 lb) sweet, ripe red plums, quartered and pitted

250 g (8 oz) ricotta cheese

4–5 tablespoons granulated sweetener

3 eggs, separated

¼ teaspoon almond essence

4 teaspoons flaked almonds

1 tablespoon icing sugar, sifted

CARBOHYDRATE 11 g

FAT 9 g

PROTEIN 8 g

ENERGY 150 kcal/630 kJ

1 Arrange half the plums randomly over the base of a buttered and base-lined 20 cm (8 inch) springform cake tin.

2 In a bowl, mix together the ricotta, 4 tablespoons of the sweetener, the egg yolks and almond essence until smooth.

3 In a second bowl, whisk the egg whites until stiff, moist peaks form. Fold into the ricotta mixture then spoon over the plums. Sprinkle the top with the flaked almonds and bake in a preheated oven, 160°C (325°F), Gas Mark 3, for 30–35 minutes until the cake is well risen, golden brown and the centre is just set. Check after 20 minutes and cover the top loosely with foil if the almonds seem to be browning too quickly.

4 Turn off the oven and leave the cake to cool for 15 minutes with the door slightly ajar. Cool then chill well in the refrigerator.

5 Meanwhile, cook the remaining plums with 2 tablespoons of water in a covered saucepan for 5 minutes until soft. Purée until smooth, mix in the remaining sweetener if needed then pour into a small jug. Remove the tin and lining paper and transfer the cake to a serving plate. Dust the top with the sifted icing sugar and serve, cut into wedges, with the sauce.

TIP When they are in season, use fresh apricots or peaches instead of the plums.

MINI ALMOND ANGEL CAKES
with Berry Fruits

These dainty little flour-free cakes are made with whisked egg whites and sweetener, to keep the carbs as low as possible, and ground almonds.

Preparation time 15 mins
Cooking time 10 mins
Serves 6

4 egg whites
3 tablespoons granulated sweetener
50 g (2 oz) ground almonds
generous pinch of cream of tartar
15 g (½ oz) flaked almonds
400 g (13 oz) frozen mixed berry fruits
200 g (7 oz) fromage frais
1 tablespoon sifted icing sugar, for dusting (optional)

CARBOHYDRATE 8 g
FAT 9 g
PROTEIN 7 g
ENERGY 140 kcal/583 kJ

1 Lightly oil 6 sections of a deep muffin tin and line the bases with circles of greaseproof paper.

2 Whisk the egg whites until stiff, moist peaks form. Whisk in the sweetener, a teaspoonful at a time, until it all has been added and continue to whisk for a minute or two until the mixture is thick and glossy.

3 Fold in the ground almonds and cream of tartar and spoon the mixture into the sections of the muffin tin. Sprinkle the flaked almonds over the tops.

4 Cook in a preheated oven, 180°C (350°F), Gas Mark 4, for 10–12 minutes until golden brown and set. Loosen the edges of the cakes with a knife and lift them on to a cooling rack.

5 Warm the fruits in a saucepan. Arrange the angel cakes on serving plates, add a spoonful of fromage frais to each and spoon the fruits around. Dust with a little sifted icing sugar, if using.

TIP These little flour-free cakes are suitable for anyone on a coeliac diet.

Index

A
almonds: angel cakes 140
aubergines 104
	brittle 114
Amaretto: chocolate mousse
	cake 129
apples: chicken 95
artichokes: buckwheat crêpes 26
	with fennel 67
asparagus: citrus-dressed 29
	green beans 110
	scallops 59
aubergines: and almonds 104
	red peppers 111
Avgolemonon sauce 48

B
baba ghanoush: lamb 90
banana and yogurt torte: iced 134
bay cream 133
beef: daube of 86
	peppered 64
beetroot, red onion and pumpkin
	bake 30
berry fruits: almond angel
	cakes 140
black bean sauce: sesame greens 47
blackberries: floating islands 125
blood sugars 7, 8
Bloody Mary jellies 68
blue cheese: chicory 102
blueberries: pots 137
	zabaglione 124
broccoli: purple sprouting 48
brown foods 8
brûlée vanilla cheesecake 132
brunches 16–37
buckwheat crêpes 26
butternut squash: baked 44
	duck 98

C
cakes: almond angel 140
	ricotta, plum and almond 139
calamari: zarzuela 76

Calvados: chicken 95
camembert soufflé: baked 107
Campari: lambs' liver 91
capers: artichokes and fennel 67
carbohydrates 6–8
cardamom: butter 46
	and coconut syllabub 114
	lamb 88
carrots: baby 46
	baked 44
cauliflower: Du Barry soup 52
celeriac: dauphinoise 43
champagne granita 121
cheesecake: brûlée vanilla 132
chicken: Normande 95
	pot-roast 94
	tikka 62
chicory gratinée 102
chilli: bitter chocolate mouse 128
	and melon sorbet 56
chives: mushroom cups 37
chocolate: bitter chocolate
	mousse 128
	mousse cake 129
chorizo: clams 84
cinnamon: chocolate mousse 128
clams 84
clementines: mango sorbet 122
coconut: cardamom and coconut
	syllabub 114
	ice cream 120
coconut milk: mussel curry 83
cod: zarzuela 76
coffee panna cotta 130
complex carbohydrates 6–7, 8
cooking 15
courgettes: eggs 22
	frittatas 24
	and lime salad 42
	red peppers 111
crab: and ginger bisque 53
	lettuce wrappers 55
cranachan 36
cranberries: camembert 107
	venison 92

crêpes: buckwheat 26
cucumber relish 55
custard: floating islands 125

D E F
dauphinoise: celeriac 43
desserts 112–41
diets 6, 8
Du Barry soup 52
duck: oriental 98
	tea-infused 60
eating habits 10–11
eating out 15
eggs: courgettes 24
	en cocotte 21
	green bean and asparagus 110
	Moroccan 22
	mushroom cups 37
	piperade 20
	quail 29
entertaining 15
exercise 11
fennel: artichokes 67
	chicken 62
figs: baked 32
floating islands 125
fruits: berry 140
	orchard 133

G
gammon: mushroom cups 37
garlic: dauphinoise 43
ginger: bitter greens 100
	crab and ginger bisque 53
	dipping sauce 103
	lamb 88
	mussel curry 83
	neep bree 49
	rhubarb and ginger parfait 116
	scallops 59
glucose 7
glycaemic index (GI) 8–9
goats' cheese: beetroot, red onion
	and pumpkin bake 30
granola: maple glazed 33

green bean and asparagus salad: warm 110
green tea: duck 60
    melon trio 34
guinea fowl: roast 96

H I J K
ham: jambon persillé 63
herring: oatmeal and mustard-crusted 28
ice cream: banana and yogurt torte 134
    coconut 120
jambon persillé 63
jellies: Bloody Mary 68
    Pimm's 126
kaffir lime: coconut ice cream 120
kidneys 25

L
lamb: liver 91
    Moroccan 88
    rack of 90
lavender: petites crémets 117
leeks: salmon 74
lemonade: Pimm's jellies 126
lemons: artichokes and fennel 67
lentils: scallops 58
lettuce wrappers 55
limes: asparagus 29
    carrots 46
    chicken 94
    courgettes 42
    prawns 82
liver: lambs' 91
lobster 80

M
main dishes 70–111
mango sorbet 122
maple glazed granola 33
Marsala: kidneys 25
mascarpone: blueberries 137
    pears 138
melon: chilli and melon sorbet 56

melon trio 34
menus 12–13
meringues: floating islands 125
mint: courgettes 24
miso broth 54
monkfish and prawn fire pot 75
Moroccan baked eggs 22
Moroccan lamb 88
mousse: bitter chocolate 128
    chocolate mousse cake 129
Muscat wine: orchard fruits 133
mushrooms: beef 86
    cups 37
    pheasant 99
    stroganoff 106
mussels: curry 83
    zarzuela 76

N O
neep bree 49
nutmeg: dauphinoise 43
oatmeal and mustard-crusted herring 28
obesity 9–10
oranges: cheesecake 132
    lambs' liver 91
orchard fruits 133

P Q
pak choi: duck 60
pancetta: beef 86
    salmon 74
panna cotta: coffee 130
Parmesan thins 52
parsnips: baked 44
passion fruit: banana and yogurt torte 134
pastrami: piperade 20
pears: honey 138
peppers: eggs 22
    rouille 66
    timbale 111
petites crémets 117
pheasant 99
picon cheese: figs 32

pimenton: clams 84
Pimm's jellies 126
pineapples 118
piperade 20
piri-piri: prawns 18
pistachios: banana and yogurt torte 134
plums: pineapple 118
    ricotta, plum and almond cake 139
    vegetable rolls 108
pomegranates: mixed leaf salad 40
prawns 18
    miso broth 54
    monkfish 75
    sautéed 82
processed food 6, 7, 9, 10
prosciutto: trout 79
prune compote 136
pumpkin: beetroot, red onion and pumpkin bake 30
purple sprouting broccoli 48
quail eggs: asparagus 29

R
raspberries: cranachan 36
red onions: beetroot 30
refined food 6, 7, 9, 10
rhubarb and ginger parfait 116
ricotta: buckwheat crêpes 26
    plum and almond cake 139
root vegetables: baked 44
Roquefort and walnut sauce 87
rouille: red pepper 66

S
saffron: red pepper rouille 66
salads: courgette and lime 42
    green bean and asparagus 110
    horseradish-dressed 64
    mixed leaf and pomegranate 40
    pak choi 60
    Vietnamese 72
salmon: asparagus 29
    buckwheat crêpes 26
    eggs 21

grilled 74

seared 72

salsa verde: guinea fowl 96

sauces: Avgolemonon 48

baba ghanoush 90

blackberry 125

cranberry 107

gingered dipping 103

hot plum 118

plum and wasabi 108

Roquefort and walnut 87

smooth plum 139

spinach 111

tomato 78, 104

watercress beurre blanc 79

scallops: ginger 59

seared 58

sea bass 78

Serrano ham: chilli and melon

sorbet 56

sesame greens 47

shallots: lobster 80

shopping 14

side dishes 38–69

simple carbohydrates 6, 7

sorbet: mango 122

soups: crab and ginger bisque 53

Du Barry 52

miso broth 54

watercress 50

spinach: red peppers 111

starters 38–69

steak: fillet 87

strawberries: champagne

granita 121

petites crémets 117

swedes: neep bree 49

syllabub: cardamom and coconut

114

T

tamarind: prawns 82

tarragon: chicken 94

eggs 21

tea creams 136

tofu 100

tomatoes: eggs 21

herring 28

kidneys 25

Moroccan eggs 22

sauces 78, 104

sea bass 78

tropical fruits: granola 33

trout: prosciutto 79

V

vegetables: tempura 103

Vietnamese rolls 108

venison 92

vermouth: lobster 80

Vietnamese salad 72

Vietnamese vegetable rolls 108

vodka: mushrooms 106

W Y Z

walnuts: chicory gratinée 102

watercress: soup 50

trout and prosciutto 79

weight 9

white wine: jambon persillé 63

yogurt: banana and yogurt torte 134

maple glazed granola 33

watercress soup 50

zabaglione: minted 124

zarzuela 76

Acknowledgements

Photography © **Octopus Publishing Group Ltd**/Stephen Conroy
Food Styling **Sara Lewis**
Executive Editor **Sarah Ford**
Editor **Jessica Cowie**
Executive Art Editor **Karen Sawyer**
Designer **Lisa Tai**
Production Controller **Manjit Sihra**